The
ART & SCIENCE
of
MEDITATION

Edited by

L. K. MISRA, Ph.D.

Published by

**THE HIMALAYAN INTERNATIONAL INSTITUTE
OF YOGA SCIENCE & PHILOSOPHY OF USA**

ISBN: 0-89389-018-9

7-87

HIMALAYAN INTERNATIONAL INSTITUTE
OF YOGA SCIENCE & PHILOSOPHY OF USA
1505 Greenwood Road, Glenview, IL 60025

CONTENTS

CONTENTS

INTRODUCTION

This book is the second in the DAWN Series of publications from the Himalayan Institute and includes articles on those aspects of Meditation which could not be included in the first book, *The Theory and Practice of Meditation.* In the first chapter, Professor Justin O'Brien has compared the methods and theological aspects of Meditation as prevalent in East and West. In the second chapter, Dr. Rudolph M. Ballentine has discussed possible obstacles in Meditation and ways to resolve such problems. In the third chapter, Professor James Heddle has given a comprehensive description of different aspects of Meditation used in psychology, parapsychology and other sciences compared to Superconscious Meditation. In the last chapter, I have given a brief description of achievements in Meditation, as discussed in the Eastern classical text, *Yoga Sutras,* compared to modern scientific views on the advantages of Meditation.

I hope this book will give readers some new thoughts in the field of Meditation.

L. K. Misra, Ph.D.
February 10, 1976

Meditation, Contemplation and the Yoga Tradition

JUSTIN O'BRIEN, Ph.D.

"*I counsel that in the earnest exercise of mystical contemplation you leave the senses and the operations of the intellect and all things that the senses or the intellect can perceive. . . and that thine understanding being laid to rest, you ascend. . . towards Him whom neither being nor understanding can contain.*"

Dionysius the Areopagite

Justin O'Brien, Ph. D., was raised in Chicago. He studied the Classics at Notre Dame University, received an M.A. in Philosophy from St. Albert's College in Oakland, California, an M. A. in Theology from Marquette University, and Doctoraal and Ph. D. degrees in Theology from Nijmegen University, the Netherlands.

He taught Theology at Edgewood College, Madison and is presently Professor of Theology at Loyola University, Chicago. He has lectured extensively throughout the United States and has travelled and studied in India and the Middle East.

One of the co-authors of Meditation in Christianity, *Dr. O'Brien conducts Meditation courses at the Himalayan Institute and throughout the Midwest.*

America abounds with opportunities to learn meditation. Techniques indigenous to Eastern cultures have been transplanted into the West in the last ten years. Ashrams, Zen centers, Yoga societies, etc., all have sprung up on this side of the Pacific allowing one to survey the spectrum of Eastern approaches to the human mind. Even scientific research in laboratories and institutes has approved human consciousness for investigation; the journals in psychology are replete with studies on altered states of consciousness and biofeedback reports.

At the same time, Christian Churches have not ignored this phenomena. With the public interest in meditation reaching both Church and non-Church affiliated peoples, modern Christian authors have been writing more openly on this subject than in previous years. Not every Christian Church espouses meditation. Those major denominations that encourage it in a detailed and systematic manner have sponsored followers who generally live in convents, monasteries and rectories. Men and women, in other words, who are considered professionally religious are the usual practitioners.

Until recently, meditation, as far as Christians were concerned, was seen only as the duty and privilege of ministers, monks, priests and nuns. The exclusiveness is readily understandable because of the way meditation has been treated by the Churches. Some of the religious communities are designated as "Contemplative" Congregations or Orders. Those who pursued the spiritual life in these communities found that meditation and contemplation formed part of their daily regime.

In the West, for the most part, these terms—meditation/contemplation—are associated with religious meaning and overtones, whereas in the East, they convey an altogether different meaning. It is to the comparison and clarification of these meanings and their practical implications that this essay is written.

For our purposes, two representative manuals

explaining meditation/contemplation have been selected from the many volumes written within the Christian tradition. These authors will be compared with one classical meditative tradition of the East: Patanjali's *Yoga Sutras*.

Christian Meditation as Mental Prayer

Strictly speaking, there is no one homogenous meditative tradition in the Christian Churches. Each sect has its history of followers who have proven the usefulness of particular forms of meditation/contemplation for their spiritual development. The resultant effect of practicing meditation has been included as part of their religious growth. Understandably, meditation/contemplation has been placed within a theological framework. In fact, when one reads the manuals concerning the "Spiritual Life", meditation and contemplation are frequently equated with forms of prayer.

One manual by Reverend A. Tanquerey, entitled, *The Spiritual Life* used extensively in monasteries and convents in America and Europe, remarks:

> The terms meditation and mental prayer are often interchanged. When differentiated,

the former is applied to that form of mental prayer wherein considerations and reasonings predominate and which, owing to this, is called discursive meditation.[1]

A more contemporary manual, *The Theology of Christian Perfection*, written by two monks states that:

Discursive meditation can be defined as a reasoned application of the mind to some supernatural truth in order to penetrate its meaning, love it and carry it into practice with the assistance of grace. The distinguishing note of meditation is that it is a reasoned or discursive type of prayer, and therefore attention is absolutely indispensable. As soon as one ceases to reason or discurse, he ceases to meditate. He may have given way to distraction, deliberately turned his mind to something else, passed on to affective prayer or contemplation, but without discursus there is no meditation.[2]

Both manuals consider this sort of "meditation" an exercise of prayer but, more, a lower form of praying suitable for beginners on the spiritual path. Whatever method of discursive meditation or mental prayer selected is viewed only as a temporary means to spiritual progress. Beginners are cautioned that these methods may get in the way of progress. A sign of the method becoming obsolete is when the meditator enters more and more with ease into an interior conversing with God. Hopefully, the method employed will lead to this monologue-type of prayer and thus retire itself. The road to perfection, for these authors, demands that one eventually dispense with what they understand by "meditation".

These manuals are indicative of a trend from the 16th century onwards to evaluate meditational practices in terms of contributing to moral integrity. The pious development of moral virtues, rather than the pursuit of enlightenment, occupies the attention of those following these methods. The emphasis upon an ethical formation of the aspirant would necessarily place reliance upon the discursive faculty. The notion of discursiveness pertains to what the mind does in its act of cognition. The deliberate conception of ideas, the pondering of problems, the intellectual sorting out and classifying of subjects, predicates and objects—these activities comprise the notion of discursiveness. In everyday terminology, to think means to direct the mind in a discursive way. Mental prayer or meditation, according to the manuals, situates thinking in a religious context, using ideas or concepts of a religious nature.

Certainly the power of the mind in its act of cognitive reflection can include the mental desire of petitionary prayer. In this way, thinking and praying are successively joined so that one refers to this cognitive combination as mental prayer or Christian meditation. In contradistinction to this approach, Yoga meditation views the same thought processes as an intruding hindrance. For the mind to involve itself with ideas or images, however inspiring or morally appropriate, restrains the very process of meditation. Instead of cogitating about pious thoughts, Yoga meditation leads the practitioner past the boundaries of imagination and rational discourse. While the meditator associates with his mental contents, remaining within the mental field, he stays occupied with their cognitive and emotional impact. By his preoccupation with the discursive plane, he cannot know the subtler levels of his consciousness.

Keeping in mind that these manuals always place their approach to meditation within a prayer context, one can better appreciate the two following examples of methods popularly followed by many religious communities of men and women.

The first method that has influenced Christians since the sixteenth century is called *The Spiritual Exercises of St. Ignatius*. It is offered as a complete guide for achieving Christian perfection. The Exercises are divided into four weeks of meditations which are generally guided by a retreat master or director. The first week is designed to help the aspirant to purify his soul and put his life in order; the aim of the second week is to lead the soul to a greater knowledge of and love for Jesus Christ; the third week is devoted to freeing the will from the psychological obstacles which stand in the way of a generous decision to follow Christ; and the fourth week is intended to purify the heart in the highest degree from false attachments to creatures, goods, or worldly ambition and honor.

For those who are unable to follow the four week regime, an intensive eight day retreat condensing the entire method may be taken. Either selection indicates that a definite atmosphere is being created—an atmosphere that uses silence, regular eating times, and many adjustments of the overall retreat for accommodating the education, temperament, role in life, age bracket, and interests of the aspirants. While the skilled retreat master permits a flexible use of the suggestions and sketches for meditating according to the plan of St. Ignatius, there is no omission of the following key or essential meditation steps. These basic steps are four in number:

1) The aspirant begins with a preparatory prayer in which he begs that his intentions and actions be solely directed to the service and honor of the Divine Majesty.

2) He conjures in the imagination the composition of place. If the object of meditation is a biblical scene, he stirs up the appropriate images relating to that scene in order to dwell upon them; if necessary, one may, should the object of meditation be sin, fantasize ugly scenes in order to provoke a horror for sin. After a sufficient time, he petitions God for the special graces to be obtained by this meditative step.

3) The body or central portion of meditation involves the exercise of the various faculties of the soul—the memory, the intellect and the will. The memory vividly portrays the material or object to be discursively meditated upon. The intellect then reflects upon the object and discerns what practical applications to one's daily life may be drawn from this consideration. The will deliberately arouses feelings of devotion about these discursive truths or just stirs up a holy feeling or a feeling of the presence of God. With the affections amplified, one's will should now decide and carry out a practical resolution inspired by the

aforesaid process.

4) One should conclude meditation with devout colloquies with the Saints or the Godhead, and survey this entire meditative process noting its imperfections and how to improve it.

The entire period for this method may last twenty minutes or as long as an hour, depending upon one's fervor or available moments.

A similar method used by Carmelite monasteries involves a three step plan. First, the meditator introduces himself to the experience through a prayerful reading of the spiritual subject matter which, in turn, will be pondered during meditation. Second, there comes the meditation proper, i.e., an imaginative presentation of the subject matter is evoked within the mind of the aspirant. A biblical episode, for example, is reflected upon with the intention of leading one to an affective, interior conversation with God. Third, one lingers now in words and prayers of thanksgiving and petitions for the desired graces from this meditation.

These are only two of the more familiar methods that are used currently among religious communities and advocated in modified form for the Christian laity. According to the manuals surveyed, meditation may be reduced to a basic framework containing these essential parts: a consideration of some supernatural or spiritual truth; the application of that truth to one's personal life; the resolution to do something about it, in some way insert that pondered truth into one's daily habits. In the words of one author, "these three steps, we believe, are absolutely essential for true meditation".[3]

The Role of Contemplation

Christian writers portray "contemplation" as a more advanced stage than meditation. Contemplation in this tradition of spiritual development is considered a supernatural gift from God rendered gratuitously to the aspirant. The aspirant has no claim upon it nor can he induce it by his own efforts. Again, like meditation, it is understood as a form of prayer.

In order to distinguish this highest type of mental activity, the manuals accord it the name "infused contemplation". By the word "infused", the reader may separate this extraordinary type of prayer from ordinary contemplation associated with the mind's study of the fine arts or the casual observance of a sunset. Even though "infused contemplation" derives its substantial presence from God's gratuitous action—referred to as a "grace"—upon the soul, this act of contemplation takes place within the individual's cognitive faculties. Unlike meditation or mental prayer, however, which was characterized as discursive, contemplation by-passes reflective activity and becomes akin to the experience of intuition: "a simple and affectionate gaze on God or things divine."[4]

The manuals caution the faithful not to be misled by the assertion that contemplation is a form of intuition rather than a discursive activity. The human faculties of intellect and will and imagination play their respective roles but in a subtler manner than in the ordinary mental operations of reasoning. To this extent, these writers continue to remind their readers that certain Medieval spiritual authors such as Eckhart, Tauler and Ruysbroeck who insisted that the highest state of contemplation went beyond the human cognitive and affective faculties, are incorrect. Such Medieval writers, it is claimed, misunderstood the nature of the human soul and its relationship to its own faculties. The human soul or consciousness is not immediately capable of operation by itself but must function through its various faculties or powers of cognition; and these powers, in turn, require a physical organ, such as the brain, nervous system and sense organs, in order to exercise their cognitive operations.   Since these psychological relationships pertain to the very nature of the human soul, even contemplation demands the use of the soul's faculties or powers.   To say otherwise, would imply that the soul or consciousness would be in its essence always in the act of awareness.

Furthermore, the manuals are careful to insist that since the object of contemplation is the Godhead, the human faculties by themselves are incapable of apprehending such a profound object. Some condescension on the part of God must be involved if mortals are to contemplate Him. God, in His infinite mercy, bestows or infuses upon the human faculties the added capacity to reach out, as it were, to an object that normally exceeds their field of operation.   In this way, the divine bestowal or grace makes the act of "infused contemplation" not a natural act of human cognition but a supernatural act, an act that is above and beyond the normal range of human endeavor.

Contemplation may only be performed on God's terms. The contemplative act of awareness remains irreproachably outside of man's finest capacities.

Within the field of "infused contemplation", the authors indicate various stages of absorption or expansive degrees. In these higher states of absorption, God has infused new ideas which represent divine truths much more clearly and impressively than before. The mind becomes increasingly enraptured with them. Love for them grows accordingly. Making these truths its own, the mind has a kind of experimental knowledge about the ultimate reality.

It is important to note that none of the manuals for one moment would admit a direct and immediate contact with God. The contemplative experience is always a mediated knowledge of God, i.e., a knowledge of sublime ideas regarding God and divine things, gratuitously implanted into the human mind by God. The reason for this impassable chasm between the aspirant and God is that only after physical death can one come into direct contact with the living God. Theologians refer to this extraordinary event as the "Beatific Vision". Short of death it is humanly impossible for contemplative persons to attain this divine experience.

Meditation in Yoga: a Comparison

The term "meditation" in yogic writings possesses an entirely different meaning and use than in the Christian manuals. It is not employed in any religious context nor does it presuppose any particular theological framework. Similar to the manuals it directs its techniques to a practical goal. Instead of concentrating on the moral growth of the individuals, which is only a part of the preparation for meditation, Yoga meditation strives to transform the individual by expanding his awareness. This enlargement is not an increase nor refinement of ideas or images but a systematic inner experiencing of richer levels of knowing reality.

In his *Yoga Sutras*, Patanjali classifies the centuries old experimental tradition of yoga meditation both as a conscious state of being and as a process that leads to the intended state. The goal of the meditator is to perdure in the state; one does not outgrow this accomplishment but deepens it increasingly.

In his analysis of human consciousness there is a distinction between this non-imaginative and non-conceptual state of consciousness and the expression of this same consciousness in its conjunction with the human body. Consciousness ordinarily utilizes the body as its instrument. The combined psycho-physical acts of sensations, imaginations and conceptualizations mediate the customary knowledge of the external world. The physical body is the organic correlate to the mental operations of consciousness. These various mental operations are collectively referred to

as the *antahkarana*.   So far the psychosomatic
structure found in the *Sutras* would be amenable
to the manuals' outline of the body-mind com-
plex.   Yet, there is a major difference between
the manuals and the *Sutras*.   The manuals insist
that the soul or consciousness in itself is inactive
or passive, that it can not perform cognition without the instrumentality of the mental faculties
being stimulated by the input from the external world.   By contrast, the *Sutras* assert that the
soul's consciousness subsists in operation, that
it never ceases to be but in a state of perfect
awareness.   While the soul may utilize the *antahkarana* or the mental faculties in conjunction with
the sense organs, there is, nevertheless, no essential dependence upon them.   In fact, through the
continual practice of yogic meditation the practitioner gradually experiences in awareness a
differentiation between the discursive contents
of his mind and his immanent act of awareness.

In the above mentioned Christian methods of
meditation, one remains within the field of his
mental faculties and dwells upon images and
ideas. Obviously these cognitive truths could very
well inspire their practical fulfillment in daily
life.   But, according to the *Sutras*, the highest
state of consciousness requires the meditator
to expand his awareness beyond the operation

of the discursive mind. For whatever is presented discursively is always rooted to the sensory data from which it arose. To this extent, the discursive mind can not help but grasp its knowable objects in a conditioned, finite, incomplete fashion. Even to speak of "infused contemplation" as the divine bestowal of ideas or truths does not allow one to exceed the internal limitations of the nature of the mind's faculties.

If there is any dependency upon the mental faculties, however subtle, the act of meditation or contemplation remains subject to the imaginative and discursive fields of finite consciousness. And even if one could still the movement of mind at the discursive level, one would then have to reckon with the surging forth of the subconscious field. In either case, concepts and memory percepts occupy the mind's attention, and the transcendental state of mystic union remains only a distant yearning.

A question arises: are the theological manuals charting the processes of meditation/contemplation as these were actually performed by Christian mystics? Or, is the theoretical scrutiny of the mystics' writings restructured into the manual form to fit with certain theological presuppositions? A certain dualism is preserved in the way the manuals treat the relationship between

the meditator and his goal, and sustained throughout the spiritual evolution to the highest state of
contemplation.   Yet the counterpoise to this
theological presupposition comes in the language
and symbolism of the mystics' writings.   St.
Teresa speaks of "an utter transformation in
God".   A Medieval work called *Theologia Ger-
manica* asks the question: "What is it to be a
partaker of the Divine Nature, or a Godlike
man? He who is imbued with the Eternal or
Divine Light and inflamed or consumed with
Eternal or Divine Love, he is a deified man and
a partaker of the Divine Nature." That the notion of "deification" is not an innovative term
spun out of the hallucinations of some obscure
but overzealous believer, there are similar cita-
tions throughout the centuries.   The Church
Father, St. Athanasius remarks in speaking of
the purpose of the Incarnation of the Word of
God, "He became man that we might become
God".   In the words of Eckhart: "If I am to
know God directly, I must become completely
He and He I: so that this He and this I become
and are one I".   A Medieval mystic, Richard
of St. Victor speaks of deification as when the
soul "is plunged in the fire of divine love, like
iron, it first loses its blackness, and then growing to white heat, it becomes like unto the fire

itself. And lastly, it grows liquid, and losing its nature is transmuted into an utterly different quality of being."

From this brief survey, the description of the ultimate attainment by those who had reached it reveals less of a duality than a unitive state of being. These meditative seekers of the transcendent absolute describe the consummation of their quest in the language of a transforming union, so far above the imagination of orthodox believers as to scandalize them. While their metaphors and analogies may differ according to their cultural background, temperaments, and tastes, there is a fixed conviction running through their writings, namely, that of man's latent absoluteness, expressed under a multitude of varied symbols. This absoluteness transcends the discursive faculties, expanding the meditator's awareness into the pure, unstructured experience of infinite consciousness. Meditation and union with reality become one. As the Christian mystic, Ruysbroeck says, "Thus do we grow and, carried above ourselves, above reason, into the very heart of love, there do we feed according to the spirit; and taking flight for the Godhead by naked love, we go to the encounter of the Bridegroom, to the encounter of His Spirit, which is His love; and thus we are brought forth by God, out of our selfhood, into the immersion of love, in which we possess blessedness and are one with God."

The poetic quality of his language is distilled by the more abstract and metaphysical terminology in Patanjali, where the goal of meditation is described as self-realization. The yogic meditator like the Christian meditator expands to the inexhaustible state of infinite knowledge; his soul or individual consciousness is engulfed by the absolute cosmic consciousness. Certainly in the beginning there appears a similar dualism between the yogic meditator and his experience of meditating. As the meditator continues his inner practices, the dawning intuition reveals that mind and body, spirit and matter, inner reality and outer reality are only apparently separated. What has started out as obviously dual at the sense and mental levels, recedes into an unparalleled unity at the absolute state of blissful or blessed awareness.

If one may compare the East and West as we have done, then certain revisions may be advanced. The manuals' treatment of meditation is improperly limited. The imagination and discursive activity of mental prayer by its own standards retains the practitioner within the sensory and conceptual field of awareness.

Reaching God or a transcendental state is prevented by the very instructions given for the activity. Christian contemplation being akin to intuition although, as the manuals understand it, still using the mental faculties, likewise keeps the aspirant from any transcendental experience. Yet the evidence of authentic transcendental states in the Christian tradition can be found by examining the lives and texts of the mystics' writings themselves. In comparison, the manuals measure their acceptable interpretation of these writings by certain psychological and theological criteria, which do not seem to do full justice to the evidence.

These criticisms aside, if one could accept Underhill's definition of mysticism as "the art of union with Reality"[5] then an unexpected convergence arises: for this definition equally spells out the meaning of yoga. A further probing may even reveal that the underlying principles of both traditions are essentially the same.

1. Tanquerey, A., O.P., *The Spiritual Life*, Trans by H. Branderis, Benziger Brothers, Boston, 1930, p. 32.

2. Royo, A. O.P. and J. Aumann, O.P., *The Theology of Christian Perfection*, The Priory Press, Dubuque, Iowa, 1962, p. 514.

3. *Ibid.* p. 519

4. *Ibid.* p. 605.

5. Underhill, Evelyn, *Practical Mysticism*, E. P. Dutton & Co., New York, 1915, p. 3.

Obstacles in Meditation

RUDOLPH M. BALLENTINE JR., M.D.

Rudolph M. Ballentine was born in 1941 in Columbia, South Carolina.   A physician and psychiatrist, he studied psychology in the United States and France before receiving his M.D. degree from Duke University. He completed a residency and was professor of psychiatry at Louisiana State University.   He then travelled widely in India learning the deeper aspects of yoga and studying Ayurvedic Medicine and Homeopathy.   He knows several languages including Hindi.

A private practitioner of General and Psychosomatic Medicine, he is the Director of the Biofeedback-Meditation and Combined Therapy Programs of the Himalayan Institute's National Headquarters. Dr. Ballentine lectures extensively around the country and is the author of Diet and Nutrition *and* Science of Breath.

For each person the obstacles encountered during the practice of meditation are different; for some people they are social, for others, physical, while for others their obstacles are primarily emotional.

Probably the first and most obvious problem that one will encounter is a physical one. "I have a headache, . . . I feel terrible, . . . my stomach is upset, . . . my back hurts, . . . so I can't do meditation." Another problem is with regulating the breath—not as commonly recognized as physical problems but important. Thoughts are also an obstacle. "I can't control the thoughts. . . too many thoughts come into my head. . . I don't know how to handle all these thoughts." People become defensive if you say they have "mental problems" though, of course, all of us do. Perhaps it is better to say, "problems with the mind", problems with regulating, controlling and directing the flow of thoughts. Some people also have difficulty in developing a clear enough idea of where meditation should lead. They are not sure how to find some direction to follow during their meditation. Then there are problems which we think of as psychosocial: "I wish I could do meditation, but my husband thinks it is ridiculous, so I just can't", or "I really want to try meditating but when you have three kids, you know, it just isn't possible." Or, another complaint, "I know it is important, but my job takes up all my time and I never have any left." Then there are emotional problems, which become obstacles for many people.

Finally dietary problems should be mentioned: There are often problems with regulating one's daily schedule in such a way that there is a time when he physiologically feels like meditating. One doesn't feel like meditating when he's starving to death; all his thoughts will be on food, he will "meditate" on food. At the other extreme, it's very difficult to do meditation after just having put food in the stomach. In this case one's consciousness is in the belly—at least it *should* be in order to properly digest the food. Since this is the grossest or crudest level of functioning—the physical material—the obstacles created here, for instance by over-eating, are the most cumbersome. But at the same time they are the most obvious, the easiest to understand and the simplest to correct.

Obstacles Arising from Dietary Habits

If the body is occupied with digestion, it is difficult to do meditation. Consciousness has the clarity and freedom to explore within only when one's system has finished with the major part of the digestive process. It becomes important, then, to find a time when one has not recently eaten to sit for meditation. Unfortunately many people find that if they must wait three to four hours after eating to meditate, they never find any time at all, because they never go longer than that without putting something into their sto-machs. But ideally, about 3 or 4 hours should be allowed to elapse after eating before attempt-ing to sit. One must find a time when the body is nourished but not loaded, when he doesn't feel hungry and yet doesn't feel full. The kind of food eaten is very relevant here. If something very heavy is eaten, it takes a long time to di-gest and it will be a longer time before one re-gains maximum clarity and alertness. If one

eats heavily consistently and often, he will probably never feel like meditating. A little knowledge of which foods digest quickly and will
soon leave one ready to do meditation and which
foods take a long time allow one to plan. This
is a practical matter and some understanding of
what will happen after different kinds of foods
are eaten is very useful. Juices take the shortest
time to digest. As far as solid foods go, fruits
digest most quickly. If one eats a meal of fruit,
within two hours he will usually feel empty again,
unless he eats a tremendous quantity. But if
most people eat their usual bulk of food in
fruits, within approximately two hours the
stomach will be empty. Vegetables, like salads,
are digested a little less quickly. Next come
cooked vegetables, of which one will take a much
larger quantity, because they are cooked down,
condensed and become heavier. They will ordinarily digest somewhat more slowly than salads.
Grains can take quite a bit more time.* After
grains, comes protein foods, cheese, meats, le-
gumes, nuts, etc. The last thing on the list is
fats, because fats take a very long time to digest.
If anything on this scale is eaten with fat added
to it, the time can be doubled. In combining

* This depends a great deal on the person. These are relative
times which are approximately accurate for most people. One's
digestive capacity and hunger can have a great influence. Quantity
is also extremely important.

the foods the picture becomes much more complicated. Emotional upsets, tension and the state of mind all affect the digestion. Moreover many people actually eat more when they are nervous, while they are actually able to handle less.

With this rough idea of the relative length of time it takes for different foods to be digested, the intake of food can be regulated in such a way that one will be physiologically ready to do meditation at the same time when he is otherwise free to do so. If one has his whole schedule arranged to do meditation at 10:30 at night and then upon sitting down he is so full of food that he falls asleep, his efforts are wasted.

Aches and Pains as an Obstacle

The next kind of obstacle that we will encounter is on a little less gross level than food but still has to do with the physical body. This set of problems is based on physical aches and pains. These are very common problems. Most people who have attempted meditation have, at some point, encountered such a difficulty. If one sits down, closes his eyes for a moment and focuses on his breathing, he can survey the body, starting with the head and proceeding down, and will find that there are parts which feel uncomfortable. This is a problem because as soon as one sits down and the ache or pain comes into focus, it pervades one's consciousness, occupies the stage of the mind so to speak. Upon opening oneself to see what can be perceived in the inner world, all that comes into awareness are these red lights flashing "pain". So the usual tendency is to get up, move around and try to forget the discomfort. The result is a harried, frenzied sort of behavior.

Trying not to be aware of the discomforts that one has makes it difficult to be open and more sensitive to the world within. A systematic approach to meditation must concern itself with what to do about aches and pains. Over thousands of years, traditional practices have been developed to deal with this. The major technique for learning how to eliminate physical aches and pains is Hatha Yoga. This includes strengthening and stretching muscles, deep relaxation, cleansing and strengthening the nervous system through breathing practices. The Hatha Yoga positions are called *asanas* in Sanskrit. *Asana* means "easy" or "comfortable". The purpose of the Hatha Yoga *asanas* is simply to enable the student to assume an easy, comfortable posture, develop a supple relaxed physical condition so that he might sit down without the distraction of aches, pains or cramps. The physical culture postures or *asanas* are designed to prepare one for the meditative *asanas*. They systematically loosen and strengthen the body so that it can assume a proper meditative position. If one has discomfort when he sits, physical postures which will help relieve that should be investigated. Muscles must be stretched and strengthened so that the body can be restored to equilibrium. It is important for such a student to experience various exercises and postures so that he can select those that seem to fit and benefit him. The next thing is to choose correctly the meditative posture itself. Even if one is in perfect health, relaxed and his body is very supple, if he sits in an awkward posture to do meditation he will soon feel aches and pains. If, for example, one sits with his head too far forward, all the muscles in the back must exert themselves in order to prevent its falling forward. These muscles overwork in such a way for awhile, but eventually they begin to go into spasm and to cramp. For such reasons the ancient teachings set down very specific instructions on the correct meditative postures. The meditative postures are those where no strain is required to keep the body in an erect position. In other words, there is complete balance. This means that the masses of weight of the body should be distributed around its axis in such a way that very little effort is required to maintain the posture. The head, chest and the hips are the three major masses of body weight. They should be arranged one above the other so they are balanced and so that the spine can serve as the central core which supports them. When there is poor alignment, muscles must over exert and tension and discomfort will result. Though one may manage to ignore the results of such poor posture, because of the preoccupations of his everyday life, when he sits for meditation, he will suddenly become aware of them. The problem seems magnified because one's preoccupation with the outside world is cut off as he turns his attention inward. Through surveying himself, he suddenly becomes aware of how poor his posture is.

The spine should be in the proper position: there is a curve inward at the neck and at the lower back, and there is a curve outward where the shoulders are. The spine is not precisely straight, like a rod, rather there should be this slight curve. When it is properly aligned in this way, the head, chest and hips are balanced one above the other.* Success in proper posture comes with constant experimentation. One must sit for some time and observe what happens when slight adjustments in position are made. As the correct posture is approached, one feels more alert and the mind becomes clearer. Often shifting position only a fraction of an inch will result in an increase in clarity of consciousness. If one assumes the best possible position each day, relaxes in it, and, day by day, gradually extends the time it is maintained, then his capacity to sit will grow. Meanwhile strength, balance and a feeling for correct alignment increase.

Once the body is relaxed and in a good posture, one becomes aware of the breath. If the breath is jerky, it can become an obstacle. This is probably much more often a problem in meditation than is realized, because many people are still preoccupied with aches, pains and postural balance, or their consciousness is still clouded by digestive overwork to allow them

---

* Westerners often find it necessary to place a cushion under the hips to get the proper positioning of the spine if they sit on the floor. Some persons may have more success by sitting in a chair, which allows the back to be comfortably erect.

to become aware of the breath. Some people
are jerky breathers, some chest breathers, and
some hold the breath intermittently. The first
step in approaching problems with breathing is to
observe one's own customary pattern of breathing.

Poorly regulated breath can be very distracting. Breathing can be an obstacle, or it can be a
tool, depending on whether or not one learns
techniques for working with it. It can be a tool
that will help in eliminating and controlling
other obstacles, especially emotional problems.
Many people encounter difficulty in meditation
because of their emotions. Emotional turmoil
stirs up one's entire physiology. When he
becomes emotional, the breath becomes irregular. This in turn affects many other systems.
Food cannot be properly digested. Tension
develops, aches and pains are accentuated. Loss
of emotional control reflects on the physical,
mental and energy levels, especially the latter.
The whole flow of energy or *prana* in the body
is disrupted.

Emotions are "felt", though not in terms
of such senses as taste, touch or smell. Rather
there is a feeling of intensity in different parts
of the body. Emotions create in the heart area,
especially, a sort of concentration of energy and

awareness. The flow of energy in the body thus shifts and can be totally disrupted and disorganized by such emotional turmoil. When this occurs, the energy is not only stirred up, it is expended. With anger, for instance, energy is rapidly dissipated and wasted. It is as though it were"poured down the drain." Extreme anger will often be found to be followed by shakiness, weakness and lethargy. In one fell swoop a person's energy is discharged, leaving him depleted. After this, meditation will be disappointing. Perhaps one's mind returns to his anger and retorts he should have made ("Next time I am going to remember to say. . . " etc.) Then the anger returns and increases and more energy is lost. Or, if one manages to get his mind off the anger, he is likely to fall asleep because of the exhaustion that follows the upset. In order to avoid having an emotional situation get out of control, one can work with the breath. Breath and emotions bear a very close relationship to each other. It is perhaps impossible to say whether the breathing difficulty causes the emotional turmoil or whether the emotional turmoil causes breathing difficulties. In a sense, both are the case because they function in an interrelated way. So when the emotions get out of control, then the breathing gets out of control, but if control of the breathing is reestablished, then the emotions calm down or if control of the emotions is reestablished, then the breathing calms down. Whereas control of the emotions may seem difficult, regulation of the breath is direct and simple. All that is necessary is to observe the breathing pattern, find out how it is irregular and return it to regularity. This doesn't mean one should eliminate emotions. They are a useful part of the personality. Just as controlling the diet doesn't mean fasting, control of the emotions doesn't mean having none.

Here we should mention those obstacles that are usually thought of as psycho-social, or problems with other people. Most problems that we encounter with other people are really not problems in others, they are problems in us and reflect our inability to regulate ourselves within. So we choose someone outside as a target to blame, such as our children, "I just had a terrible time with the kids all day. By the time it's evening and I could do meditation, I am just exhausted." This matter is very much related to emotions and breathing. Coping with one's children can be exhausting or exhilarating, depending upon his attitude toward them. One will find in his personal experience that there are some kinds of work where the more work he does the more energy he has. There are other situations where after a few hours he feels exhausted. Which one occurs is not so much a matter of the muscle power used, or the number of brain cells operating, it has more to do with one's reasons for acting, and what it means to him. One attitude toward work will lead to such a state that one can sit down and slip easily into a meditative state. The other kind will lead one to such a state that any attempt at meditation ends only with sleepiness and frustration.

Once the body is comfortable, free from aches and pains and not overloaded with food or complaining with hunger; once the breath is regulated, a new set of obstacles becomes apparent: these have to do with annoying, persistant and distracting thoughts. What to do with thoughts? Many students of meditation rank as their major obstacle "trouble thoughts". How can these be handled? What is to be done with them? If he calms the body and makes the breath regular, the student begins to find himself aware of only thoughts, and he begins to wonder what else he could be aware of; after all, isn't the mind simply a flow of thoughts? If one is to limit himself to this inner world of endless and often monotonous thoughts, how can he be anything but bored?

This raises a question occasionally asked by students: "Where is meditation supposed to lead anyhow?" What direction should it take? We must deal with this question before we can understand how to cope with thoughts. Most of us tend to think of ourselves as more or less identical with our minds, with the set of mental habits that come into prominence when we sit quietly. At the same time, of course, it is this set of mental habits which limits us, confines us, and prevents our growth and personal evolution. The basic purpose of meditation is to help us step beyond this circle of thoughts, to escape the repetitive chain of mental events that has us trapped. "What? Stop thinking? Impossible!" This is our initial response to the proposition. Our identity *is* our thoughts, so the idea of going beyond them seems strange. Yet the purpose of meditation is to expand awareness beyond the limits of "thinking", enlarging our field of awareness to include other non-verbal, "non-mental" areas of consciousness. Thoughts do not disappear. They remain active and visible in one corner of our consciousness. But they cease to be the totality of our awareness. Our choices and our creativity are multiplied and enhanced by escaping the limitations of our thoughts. So meditation should lead beyond the "mind".

When one grasps this, he suddenly becomes aware of the difficulty in carrying it out. "Am I going beyond my thoughts?" he thinks busily, or "I'm not going to think about that, I'm not going to think about anything, because. . . etc." So the student realizes with exasperation that he is simply thinking about not thinking! It seems an endless cycle. It's like quicksand, every attempt to push oneself free only results in sinking deeper.

It is for this reason that students are often prescribed a sound on which they can focus. This, when properly selected by the teacher, permits them to turn their attention to something which is outside the circle of thoughts. A sort of "place to stand" in the inner world, from which the thoughts can be surveyed without being entangled in them. This sound focus which is used almost universally in meditation is called in Sanskrit *mantra*. The task of the student becomes one of holding the attention on it and avoiding the tendency to slip back, and lose himself in thought.

Once again, the breath becomes very important, since each time the flow of breath is interrupted, attention is jostled and shifts. If the breath is perfectly smooth, concentration can be held on the *mantra* and consciousness can rise to a point from which much more is included in the field of awareness. But when the breath is interrupted, so is this expanded awareness, and a jerky series of thoughts comes once more to dominate consciousness.

Over the ages, each of the obstacles encountered by man in his search for expanded consciousness has been identified, struggled with, and overcome. The techniques necessary for the conquest of these obstacles have been repeatedly described and taught to devoted and sincere students. What remains is only for the student to make a consistent, alert, and adventurous application of the methods. Then the obstacles fade, one by one, into obscurity. As the obstacles disappear, consciousness rises, as is its natural tendency, towards fuller and more evolved states.

Science and the Superconscious

Twentieth Century Worldviews and the Meditative Tradition

JAMES HEDDLE, M.A.

"This is the only way, O Monks, to explain existence, to overcome sadness and misery, to find the right path, to realize nirvana—it is correct meditation. Everything points to this, and to this alone." Thus spoke the enlightened. The monks rejoiced at his words.

Sutta Pitaka

James Heddle was born in Detroit in 1940. He received his A.B. degree from Albion College and Wayne State University and an M.A. in Urban Sociology from Wayne State. He studied film for a year at the London School of Film Technique, and later worked as a film-maker in Detroit and a producer of Educational Film at the University of Wisconsin in Madison. He worked as a race-relations professional in Detroit and as a social worker in the Bronx, New York.

For three years he taught Film-making and Inter-Media Studies at the University of Wisconsin, Madison, and is presently teaching Inter-Media and Future Studies at William James College, Grand Rapids, Michigan.

Science and spirituality have long been thought to be mutually exclusive, even opposing, modes of human knowing. This idea still obtains widely despite the fact that in our heavily scientized society, there is unprecedented popular interest in the varieties of spiritual culture. In what follows the relationship between these two approaches to the person and to the world will be explored.

Concensual Reality and the Perennial Philosophy

Evolving Western science has found it necessary to revise and discard, often repeatedly, its most cherished ideas concerning the nature and operation of the various classes of phenomena to which it has addressed itself. Every science at a given time in its development, holds to a certain organizing image of its subject matter which accounts for most of the known facts and focusses further research.   Such an organizing image or "paradigm" often acquires the compelling force of belief or even of dogma for scientists within its field and blinds them to data which contradict it (Kuhn, 1970). As William Blake put it, "We can only perceive or sense what we are capable of imagining." The accumulation of contradictory data must be massive indeed before an image change or paradigm shift occurs to account for it.

In this section we will look briefly at several recent paradigm shifts which are crucial to our study, and which are profoundly affecting the concensual image of 'reality' itself in the closing quarter of this century. The shifts we will consider are occurring in the areas of psychology, biology, physics and psychiatry.

Psychology
William James: Beyond the Screen

As the Twentieth Century opened, the dominant thrust of establishment science was to explain human consciousness as a fortuitous function—a sort of accidental excrescence—of an unconscious universe conceived of as a grand machine. There were, of course, dissenting voices and contrary signs which would have to wait to be heard and read (Grun, 1975). Henri Bergson was developing his philosophy of organic evolutionism which was soon to find echos in the work of the Indian Yogi Aurobindo and the French Jesuit Teilhard. Ruldoph Steiner was founding anthroposophy. Max Planck was formulating quantum theory, and Einstein the Special Theory of Relativity, two of the key developments leading to today's "mystical" physics which will be touched on below. The genetic findings of Gregor Mendel were rediscovered after twenty years of being ignored. Transatlantic radio-telegraphy, magnetic recording of sound, the invention of the arc generator, and the first powered airplane flight were initiating the era of electricity, electronic communications and global transportation, and thus the planetary intermingling of people, cultures, and ideas which we now take for granted. The Russian psychologist Pavlov was exploring the influence of the mind on the body with his study of "conditioned reflex"; and in Edinburgh the American psychologist William James was delivering the Giford Lectures on natural religion which would later be published as the classic *Varieties of Religious Experience.* Buried in that work was a prophetic paragraph which was to emerge seventy years later as the virtual credo of scientific consciousness research. James said, referring to his experiments with his own consciousness,

> One conclusion was forced upon my mind. . . and my impression of its truth has ever since remained unshaken. It is that our normal consciousness, rational consciousness as we call it, is but one special type of consciousness, whilst all about it, parted from it by the filmiest of screens, there lie potential forms of consciousness entirely different. We may go through life without suspecting their existence; but apply the requisite stimulus, and at a touch they are there in all their completeness, definite types of mentality which probably somewhere have their field of application and adaptation. No account of the universe in its totality can be final which leaves these other forms of consciousness quite disregarded. How to regard them is the question—for they are so discontinuous with ordinary consciousness. Yet they may determine attitudes though they cannot furnish formulas, and open a region though they fail to give a map. At any rate, they forbid premature closing of our accounts with reality. (James, 1958, p.298).

This is the first unequivocal statement in main stream western psychology of an attitude that was to lead to the scientific corroboration of the validity and universality of types of experiences shared by individuals in all spiritual traditions.

A researcher ahead of his culture, William James embodied in his personal interests and in his work virtually all the subjects that have become the key areas of inquiry for the growing edge of contemporary psychology. One of these was the area of psychical research or parapsychology. Summing up his researches in 1909, James again took an unequivocal position against the mainstream view. "I wish to go on record," he said, "for. . . *the presence,* in the midst of all the humbug, *of really supernormal knowledge.*" (His emphasis. Quoted in Mishlove, 1975, p.103).

Parapsychology

It was not until 1970, with the publication of Ostrander and Schroeder's *Psychic Discoveries Behind the Iron Curtain,* that more than a few American Scientists, and U. S. culture generally, began to take "paranormal" phenomena as seriously as James had in 1909 (Moss, 1974). It is in the light of the work of such respected scientists as J. B. Rhine, Charles Tart, Elmer & Alyce Green, Stanley Kripner, Thelma Moss, Stanislov Grof, John Lilly, and Edgar Mitchell that the current widespread interest in spiritual culture must in part be considered. Reports of telepathic communication clairvoyance (sensing of events at a distance), psychic diagnosis and healing, mental precipitation or transformation of physical objects, psychokenesis (the non-physical movement of physical objects), pre-cognition (psychic foreknowledge of events), out-of-body experiences (astral travel) and other "occult" phenomena have long been an integral part of the traditional wisdom systems of east and west. (Yogananda, 1972 and Ram Dass, 1974). In fact, it is such elements which have been the chief targets of derision from those operating within the belief system of 19th and early 20th century science. During the last decade, however, this category of events has come to be the focus of much carefully controlled research in laboratories on both sides of the Iron Curtain.

The work of Elmer and Alyce Green of the Menninger Foundation has been pivotal to the shift in attitude of western scientists toward these formerly taboo areas of inquiry. Their contributions in several contexts will be referred to below. The Greens were considerably aided by their collaboration in the early 70's with Swami Rama, perhaps the first master yogi to submit himself rather than his students to the rigors of

systematic laboratory testing. Here is the Greens'
description of one of their research sessions as
reported in the *World Book Encyclopedia:*

> Seated in a chair in our laboratory at the Men-
> ninger Foundation in Topeka, Kansas, a 45-
> year-old Indian yogi named Swami Rama per-
> formed an incredible feat.[1] While seven of us
> watched, the Swami caused a 14-inch aluminum
> knitting needle, mounted horizontally on a
> vertical shaft five feet away from him to rotate
> toward him through 10 degrees of arc. The
> Swami had been fitted with a plastic mask that
> covered his nose and mouth. He breathed
> through a foam-rubber insert which was covered
> by a plexiglass shield to deflect "air currents"
> down to the sides. Even with this, one of the
> observers was convinced that the Swami had
> used some method that could be explained
> by some already known physical law.
>
> We had warned the Swami that even if he
> succeeded in demonstrating this kind of phe-
> nomena not everyone would accept his expla-
> nation of how he had done it. He replied,
> "That's all right. Every man can have his own
> hypothesis, but he still has to account for the
> facts." (Green and Green 1974, pp. 137-8).

Elsewhere the Greens have observed (1971-A):

> In our research with the Swami we naturally
> focused a good deal of attention on physiological
> data because they are easy to put into graphical

form, and it is easier to get research money for
projects that come out with red ink on green
graph paper. Some of Swami Rama's other
accomplishments were of utmost interest,
however. For instance, we observed that he
could diagnose physical ailments very much in
the manner of Edgar Cayce, except that he
appeared to be totally conscious, though
with indrawn attention for a few seconds while
he was "picking up" information. (p. 24-5).

In the thirties and forties J. B. Rhine and
his associates at Duke University labored virtually alone in rigorous statistical experiments
aimed at demonstrating to an often hostile
scientific community that ESP, meaning clairvoyance, telepathy, and precognition, existed as
an actual class of phenomena beyond the limits
of mere chance occurrence. Now, in the seven-
ties, researchers securely within the range of
"normal sciences" (Kuhn, 1970) are studying
a wide variety of psychic, or "psi", phenomena not to prove their existence—which is taken
for granted—but to find out how they work.

While the study of psi functions is irrelevant
and indeed inimical to the serious study and
practice of meditation and related disciplines,
their acceptance as valid subjects for scientific investigation is a major step in the revision

of the Western worldview and an important factor in the rapprochement of traditional teachings and contemporary thought. Let us consider some others.

Biofeedback

The notion of a split between mind and body, long an unquestioned item of belief in western psychology, was thrown in serious doubt by the work of Freud and Pavlov, laid to rest by the development of psychosomatic medicine and erased by the reductionist approach which saw mind as an accidental result of physio-chemical stimulus-response activity. It was replaced by the belief in the paired dichotomies of conscious/unconscious and central nervous system/autonomic nervous system, the central nervous system—brain and spinal cord—operating "input" (sensory) functions, and the "output" (muscular control) functions was said to be generally under the governance of the conscious mind. Occasionally, in conditions viewed for the most part as pathological, the central nervous system was known to come under the influence of the unconscious mind. The autonomic nervous system—nerve fibers and ganglia external to the spinal cord—operating glandular secretions, metabolic processes, heart rate, body temperature and the like—were held to be exclusively self-functioning. Except that is, in those cases, such as some forms of paralysis and psychogenic disease, where the unconscious mind seemed to exercise control (Rama, 1973). Autonomic functions were found to be subject to external, albeit still (to the subject) unconscious, control by the techniques embodied in Pavlovian "conditioned learning" and Skinnerian "operant conditioning" (Brown, 1974).

Two radical alternatives to this model of human nervous system functioning are now reinforcing each other; the yogic model and the bio-feedback model.

Until recently the phrase "mind over body" conjured up the cliche image of an eastern fakir pacing about on a bed of hot coals. Now, it is more likely to suggest the equally cliche image of a western college student festooned with electrodes meditating in a research laboratory. The reason for this is the virtual explosion of research in the area of biofeedback (Brown and Klug, 1974). It has been made possible by the development of electronic technology that enables a researcher to monitor minute physiological changes in the body of a human subject. When the resulting information on subtly changing internal states is "fed back" to the subject via light or sound patterns, he or she can learn with practice to voluntarily control these internal changes. The limits of such control have not yet been defined experimentally and extend to voluntary changes in heartrate, temperature, muscle tension, glandular secretion, brain wave activity, and beyond.

> The demonstration by Basmajian and others that human beings can voluntarily control the electrical activity of *a single motoneuron cell in the spinal cord* would seem to be the ultimate voluntary control over the body. Speculation suggests that the ultimate lies further beyond this. (Brown, 1974, p.391. My emphasis).

All of this of course comes as no surprise to accomplished practitioners of Yoga, who have been engaging in the voluntary control of internal states for millennia—without the aid of electronics.

An important confluence of the eastern and western approaches to voluntary internal controls was again embodied in the collaboration between bio-feedback researcher Elmer and Alyce Green and yoga master, Swami Rama. In order to preserve the flavor of these experiments, I will not attempt to summarize, but present portions of Dr. Green's narration itself. The longest series of experiments, conducted at the Menninger Foundation in 1970, were "especially for correlating internal psychological states (phenomenological or existential states) with brain wave patterns." The immense environmental differences between the Himalayan cave where the Swami had perfected his internal control techniques and the scientific laboratory where he was now called upon to demonstrate them need hardly be stressed. After a period of adjustment, however, the Greens and their associate Dale Walters, found Swami Rama

> able to enter various states (evidenced by remarkable changes in brain wave patterns) in no more than fifteen minutes, and usually in five minutes.
>
> In five 15-minute brainwave feedback sessions he was able to tie together in his mind the relationship between the tones produced by activation in the various brain wave bands and the states of consciousness he had learned in a Himalayan cave. Then he produced 70% alpha waves over a five-minute period of time by thinking of an empty blue sky 'with a small white cloud' sometimes coming by. After a number of alpha-producing sessions the Swami said, 'I have news for you, alpha isn't anything. It is literally nothing.' This did not surprise us, because we had already observed that the best way to produce alpha was to close the eyes and think of nothing in particular but it would have provided a shock, I suppose, to the many mind-training researchers who are

telling people all over the country that when in the alpha brainwave state you can get rid of your diseases, get the most wonderful ideas, and best of all be telepathic. . .

In any event, the Swami next produced theta waves by 'stilling the conscious mind and bringing forward the unconscious.' In one five minute period of the test he produced theta waves 75% of the time. I asked him what his experience was and he answered that it was an unpleasant state, 'very noisy.' The things he had wanted to do but did not do, the things he should have done but did not do, and associated images and memories of people who wanted him to do things, came up in a rush and began shouting at him. It was a state that he generally kept turned off, he said, but it was also instructive and important to look in once in a while to see what was there. (pp. 21-2)

. . . After producing theta waves, the Swami said he knew exactly how the inner states of awareness were arranged in respect to brain wave frequency bands. Then he said, 'tomorrow I will consciously make delta waves for you.' I replied that I doubted that he would succeed in that because he would have to be sound asleep to produce delta. He laughed at this and said that I would think that he was asleep but that he would be conscious of everything that occurred in the experimental room.

Before this test he asked how long I would like to have him remain in the delta state. I said that 25 minutes would be all right and he said he would bring himself out at that time. After about five minutes of meditation, lying down with his eyes shut, the Swami began producing delta waves, which we have never before seen in his record. In addition, he snored gently. Alyce, without having told Swami that she was going to say anything. . . then made a statement in a low voice, . . . Every five minutes she made another statement in a low voice and after 25 minutes had passed the Swami roused himself and said that some one with sharp heels had walked on the floor above and made a click, click, click noise during the test, and a door had been slammed twice somewhere in the building and that Mrs. Green had said—and here he gave her statements verbatim, except for the last half of the fourth sentence, of which he had the gist correct though not the words. I was very much impressed because in listening from the control room, I had heard her sentences, but could not remember them all, and I was supposed to have been awake. (Green, 1971, pp. 21-3).

[In other experiments Swami Rama] made the temperature of the little finger side of his right palm differ from the temperature of the thumb side by 10 degrees F. He did this apparently by controlling the flow of blood in the large radial and ulnar arteries of his wrist. Without moving or using muscle tension, he 'turned on' one of them and 'turned off' the other. Later, he demonstrated that he could stop his heart from pumping blood. . .

We asked the Swami how he controlled his heart and blood vessels, and how he consciously produced various kinds of brain waves at will. He explained that these phenomena were possible because, *All of the body is in the mind. But,* he added, *not all of the mind is in the body.'* (Green, 1974, pp. 142-3, My emphasis).

The importance of Swami Rama's demonstrations did not lie in the performances themselves but in their implications. I do not intend to practice stopping my heart or to try to teach anyone else according to the Swami's instructions, but the fact that *it can be done* is of major scientific importance. (Green, 1971a p. 19. His emphasis).

As a result of these and other experiments on body-mind interaction, the Greens have postulated the so-called *Psycho-physiological Principle* which reads: 'Every change in the physiological state is accompanied by an appropriate change in the mental-emotional state, conscious or unconscious, and, conversely, every change in the mental-emotional state, conscious or unconscious, is accompanied by an appropriate change in the physiological state.' (Ibid. p. 14). They further explain that

. . . the psycho-physiological principle, or its expression in the psychosomatic unity of mind and body, is manipulated by volition which at

present is of indeterminate origin, but which at
least exhibits some of the characteristics of meta-
force [i.e., a 'force' transcendant to the mind-
body system itself]. These ideas, incidentally,
are quite clearly put forth in the Vedas, sacred
scriptures of India, and lie behind the system
of Raja Yoga.

Thus the findings of bio-feedback research,
like those of parapsychology, lead scientists—one
wants to say inexorably—toward a concept of
"mind-at-large" or a general "field theory" of
consciousness in which, as Swami Rama has
phrased it, "All of the body is in the mind.
But not all of the mind is in the body". Formulating this in their own way, the Greens
paraphrase yogic theory to suggest that

> . . . The body is only the densest section of a
> 'field of energy' that includes both body and
> mind. It is interesting to remember that our
> bodies, like everything else in the universe, are
> electromagnetic fields with swarms of particles as
> dense portions. We are almost entirely empty
> space, although we see ourselves and all nature
> as solid matter *because that is the way we were
> constructed by evolution to see.*
>
> . . . For the mind is an energy structure, and all
> matter, whether physiological or nonphysiological,
> is a matrix of energy that is somehow related to
> mind. *In every thought and in every cell, we are
> part of the general field,* but we are normally un-

aware of this because we are not conscious of our
own unconscious. (Green and Green, 1974, my
emphasis).

That such a statement can appear matter-of-
factly in the pages of a popular, mass-produced
encyclopedia is in itself an index of the remark-
able confluence of traditional mystical teachings
and the growing edge of 20th century science.
But it is by no means the only one, as we shall see
below.

Alyce and Elmer Green were part of a group
of scientists who, beginning in 1969, organized
a yearly research gathering at Council Grove,
Kansas called the Interdisciplinary Conference
on Voluntary Control of Internal States. The
assemblies have had as their aim the removal
of barriers to the development of a science of
ultimate states and values—the creation of a
"new experiential/experimental. . . Science
of Consciousness". (Weide, 1972).

At Council Grove IV, held in April of 1972,
the participants agreed in part that "What makes
old ideas new is taking them seriously. . . " and
that the contemporary scientist of consciousness ". . . should read the 'scientific journals'
(i.e., great spiritual systems) of other cultures.
The Science of Consciousness has already been

written." (Ibid. p. 84, my emphasis).

The influence of such events on the worldview of society at large is slow to emerge. But at least one writer (Harman, 1972) has suggested that the ultimate impact of such findings will be of a significance equal to the 17th century rediscovery that the earth revolves around the sun. He has dubbed these changes in scientific theory 'The New Copernican Revolution'.

Biology

One night in 1966 a prominent teacher of lie-detector techniques named Clive Backster responded to an impulse and connected the electrodes of his polygraph machine to a plant in his office. He then gave the plant some water. The pen tracing the machine's rolling graph paper did not trend upward as he expected, indicating an increase in electrical conductivity due to the presence of water. Instead, the tracing trended downward and showed a sawtooth pattern similar to that produced by a human being experiencing a brief emotional stimulus (Tompkins and Bird, 1973).

His curiosity aroused, Backster determined to test further by injuring a leaf of the plant with a burning match. Immediately the image entered his mind, yet before he could act upon it or even move, the polygraph readout indicated a strong reaction from the plant. It was as if the plant had read his mind.

This was the beginning of a series of rigorous experiments which subsequently led Backster and other researchers to recognize the existence in plants of a telepathic sensitivity or as Backster termed it, a faculty of "primary perception." (Ibid. p.6). The plants were able to sense emotions in the human beings around them and to react to the injury or death of other organisms unconnected to them in any physical way. Not only that, but

> once attuned to a particular person, plants appeared to be able to maintain a link with that person, no matter where he went, even among thousands of people. . . [The plants of one woman] . . . remained attuned to her on a seven-hundred-mile plane ride across the United States. From synchronized clocks [experimenters]. . . found a definite reaction from the plants to the friend's emotional stress each time the plane touched down for its landing. (Ibid. p. 10).

These findings led Backster and his medical consultant, cytologist Dr. Howard Miller to hypothesize that "the five senses in humans might be limiting factors overlying a more 'primary

perception', possibly common to all nature." In
order to test for such "cellular consciousness"

> Backster found a way of attaching electrodes to
> infusions of all sorts of single cells, such as
> amoeba, paramecium, yeast, mold cultures,
> scrapings from the human mouth, blood, and
> even sperm. All were subject to being monitor-
> ed on the polygraph with charts just as interesting
> as those produced by the plants. Sperm cells
> turned out to be surprisingly canny in that they
> seemed to be capable of identifying and reacting
> to the presence of their own donor, ignoring
> the presence of other males. Such observations
> seem to imply that some sort of total memory
> may go down to the single cell, and by inference
> that the brain may be just switching mechanism,
> not necessarily a memory storage organ.
>
> 'Sentience', says Backster, 'does not seem to
> stop at the cellular level. It may go down to the
> molecular, the atomic and even the subatomic.'
> (Ibid. p. 12).

Other researchers report similar results. Bio-
chemist Sister Mary Justice Smith, a Franciscan
nun, has demonstrated that psychic healing is
testable and provable in the scientific laboratory.
Using the enzyme Trypsen, she has demonstrated
conclusively that this catalytic micro-organism,
a factor in the maintenance of the human bio-
system, responds with an increased rate of activity to the attentions of a psychic healer.

Physics

On July 16, 1945 in the desert near Alamogordo, New Mexico there occurred the detonation of the first atomic bomb. As he watched this event which so radically altered the world situation, Robert J. Oppenheimer, one of the bomb's developers, was reminded of the following words:

> "If there be the effulgence of a thousand suns bursting forth all at once in the heavens, even that would hardly approach the splendor of the mighty Lord" (Goyandka, 1973. p. 231).

It was a verse from the *Bhagavadgita*, the Third Century summation of ancient Indian Vedic philosophy.

That a 20th century atomic physicist should quote with such facility from an eastern mystical text is less surprising than it might at first seem—as the following may make clear.

Just as the paradigm of a mind-body split has had to be abandoned as a result of findings in physiological psychology and biology, so too the paradigm of spirit-matter dualism central to classical mechanistic physics since the days of Greek philosophy has gone through radical shift in our century.

The complexities and philosophical implications of contemporary physics have long been a sealed book to the layman. Thanks to the recent work of such writers as Koestler (1972), Capra (1975), LeShan (1974) Wheeler (1967, 1973), Chesterman, *et al* (1975), and Toben, Sarfatti and Wolf (1975) this is no longer the case.

The outlines of a new paradigm for physics began to emerge before 1920 with the experimental validation of Planck's Quantum theory and Einstein's Special and General Theories of Relativity. In 1919, Sir Arthur Eddington proved with photographs taken during an eclipse of the sun that the path of light passing the sun is bent by solar gravity. With this single experiment the fundamental assumptions of Euclidian geometry and Newtonian physics were knocked into a cocked hat. On November 7, 1919, the *Times* of London announced that "The scientific concept of the fabric of the universe must be changed." (Quoted in Chesterman, *et al*, 1975, p. 255). What that change might mean was soon suggested by British physicist Sir James Jeans. "The universe," he wrote,

> begins to look more like a great thought than like a great machine. Mind no longer appears as an accidental intruder into the realm of matter. We are beginning to suspect that we ought to hail it as the creator and governor of the realm of

matter. (Quoted in Hawken, p. 107).

Mechanism had been laid to rest and, despite Einstein's personal objections, the concept of determinism was soon to follow. In 1927 Werner Heisenberg published his *Uncertainty Principal* showing that no event is independent of its observer and thus setting the limits to scientific knowledge. "When we get down to the atomic level," he said, "the objective world in space and time no longer exists, and the mathematical symbols of theoretical physics refer merely to possibilities, not to facts." (Quoted in Chesterman, p. 263).

The work of Planck, Eisenstein, Minkowski, Heisenberg and many others laid the groundwork for a new 'organic' paradigm in physics which has been built upon by decades of subsequent research. It is common knowledge that this new paradigm has produced the creative/destructive power of nuclear energy. It is only beginning to be common knowledge that it has also produced a vision of the universe that is extremely close to that presented by the teachings of the East and the mystics of the West. (LeShan, 1974; Capra, 1975; Toben, Sarfatti and Wolf, 1975).

So great is this similarity that, as LeShan has demonstrated (1974), it is often impossible to distinguish the statements of mystics about the

nature of ultimate reality from those of 20th
century physicists.   Heisenberg's statement,
quoted above, could well be a definition of the
Eastern concept of *Maya* concerning the illusory
character of the perceived world. So also might
the recent statement by R. B. Fuller that

> . . . science has made no experimental finding
> of any phenomena that can be described as a
> solid, or as continuous, or as a straight sur-
> face plane, or as a straight line, or as infinite
> anything. We are now . . . forced to conclude
> that all phenomena are metaphysical; where-
> fore, as many have long suspected—like it or
> not—life is but a dream. (Fuller, 1975).

Following are some examples of interchange-
able mystic/physicist statements that tend to sup-
port Josiah Royce's opinion that mystics are "the
most thorough going empiricists in the history of
philosophy" (quoted in LeShan, 1974).   As
physicist Niels Bohr puts it, "The development of
atomic physics . . forces us to an attitude recalling
ancient wisdom . . ."(*Ibid.* p. 252).

A.   "For in the absolute, there is neither space,
      time nor causation . . . it is all one."

B.   "There is no space-time, there is not time,

there is no before, there is no after."

C. ". . . the stuff of the world is mind stuff."

D. ". . . all phenomena and their development are simply manifestations of mind. . ."

E. "It is immediately apparent, however, that this sense-world, this seemingly external universe, though it may be useful and valid in other respects, cannot be the external world, but only the self's projected picture of it. . "

F. ". . . The reason why our sentient, percipient, and thinking ego is met nowhere in our world picture can easily be indicated in seven words: because it is ITSELF that world picture. . ."

G. "No doubt we should not speak of seeing, but, instead of seen and seer, speak boldly of a simple unity. For in this seeing we neither distinguish nor are there two."

H. ". . . the vital act is the act of participation. 'Participator' is the incontrovertible new concept given by quantum mechanics. It strikes down the term 'observer' of classical theory. . ."

I.   "What is cause of this universe?. . . time,
        space, law, chance, matter, primal energy,
        intelligence—none of these, nor a combina-
        tion of these can be the final cause of the
        universe for they are effects. . . this universe
        which is made up of the perishable, the man-
        ifest and the unmanifest. . . realize that
        mind, matter, and. . . the power which u-
        nites mind and matter are but three aspects
        of. . . the one reality."

J.   "Matter expressed itself eventually as a for-
        mulation of some unknown force. Life, too,
        that yet unfathomed mystery, begins to re-
        veal itself as an obscure energy of sensitiv-
        ity imprisoned in its material formulation;
        and when the dividing ignorance is cured
        that gives us the sense of a gulf between life
        and matter will be found to be anything
        else than one energy, triply formulated."

K.   "Religion and natural science are fighting a
        joint battle in a second, never-ending crusade
        against skepticism and dogmatism, and
        against superstition. The rallying cry for
        this crusade has always been and always will

be 'On to God!' "

L.   "The external world and . . . (the). . . inner
      world are . . . only two sides of the same
      fabric, in which the threads of all forces
      and of all events, of all forms of conscious-
      ness and of their objects, are woven into an
      inseparable net of endless, mutually condi-
      tioned relations."[2]

In view of the foregoing, it comes as no surprise
that there has emerged a ". . . rapprochement between the conceptual world of parapsychology
and that of modern physics. . . " (Koestler,
1972).   According to physicist Jack Sarfatti,

> . . . mathematics is the deep language of
> transcendent experience.   The Nobel Prize
> physicist Eugene Wigner of Princeton has
> repeatedly written that consciousness is at
> the root of the quantum principle.   His
> colleague John Wheeler agrees.   Another
> Nobel Prize physicist, Brian Josephson of
> Cambridge, presents a case that the laws of
> high-energy physics as revealed in the data
> from the large accelerators may be changing
> due to the psychokinetic action of the ex-
> perimenters and theorists themselves! Fare-
> well objective Science! (in Mishlove, 1975.
> p. 228).

Psychiatry

We have seen how radical transformation of the paradigms of mind, nature and reality have produced a convergence, if not a congruence, between the world-views of several contemporary sciences and traditional "mystical" philosophies. An important area remains to be surveyed; that of psyche and self.

The mistaken dualistic vision of the world that dominated Western thought from its inception to the middle years of our century was given its most influential formulation in the writings of the 17th century French thinker Rene Descartes. As physicist Fritjof Capra (1975) has pointed out Descartes' dicotomization of the world into the separate domains of "mind" and "matter"

> ... was not only important for the development of classical physics, but has had a tremendous influence on the general Western way of thinking up to the present day. As a consequence of the Cartesian division, most Western individuals are aware of themselves as isolated egos which exist inside their bodies and are separated from the world "outside". (*Ibid.*, p. 32).

This sense of alienation of the individual "ego" from "everything-and-everybody-else" can be seen as the source of virtually all the psychopathologies that beset Western humans. It is also the dominant paradigm for "cure" in Western therapies. The psychotherapist himself was originally called an "alienist" (Watts, 1961), and the aim of most systems from psychoanalysis to "assertiveness training" is the strengthening of the ego against a spectrum of "outside" influences from "mom and dad" to "society". The "ego-psychologies" thus stand in diametric contrast to traditional growth systems which see the ego, together with the ceaseless random activity of the normal mind, as the chief barrier to "mental health", enlightenment and self-realization.

R. D. Laing gives a forceful description of the ultimate vagueness of the ego concept. He points out that

> Our society is a plural one in many senses. Any one person is likely to be a participant in a number of groups. . .
>
> Each group requires more or less radical internal transformation of the persons who comprise it. Consider the metamorphoses that one man may go through in one day as he moves from mode of sociality to another—family man, speck of crowd dust, functionary in the organization, friend. These

are not simply different roles: each is a whole
past and present and future. . .
. . . There is every temptation to start with a
notion of some supposed basic personality,
but halo effects are not reducible to one
internal system. The tired family man at the
office and the tired businessman at home
attest to the fact that people carry over, not
just one set of internal objects, but *various
internalized social modes of being,* often
grossly contradictory, from one context to
another.

Nor are there such constant emotions or
sentiments as love, hate, anger, trust or mis-
trust. . . Each emotion is always found in one
or another inflection according to the group
mode it occurs in. There are no "basic"
emotions, instincts or personality, outside of
the relationships a person has within one or
another social context. (Laing, 1967, pp.
97-98. His and my emphasis).

In recent years, a number of dissenting voices
from within the ranks of psychiatry itself have
been raised against the tyranny of the ego model.
One of the earliest of these was Carl Jung, who
postulated the existence of a " ollective unconscious" connecting all mankind below the surface, as it were, like the islands of an archipelago.
An even earlier dissenter, as we have seen, was

William James, who suggested that we construct our images of ourselves and of the world by selecting a limited number of elements from a virtually unlimited range of alternatives. "We see," he wrote,

> that the mind is at every stage a theatre of simultaneous possibilities. Consciousness consists in the. . . selection of some, and the suppression of others. . . by the reinforcing and inhibiting agency of attention. . . . Mental products are filtered from the data chosen . . . (quoted in Ornstein, 1972, p. 18).

Other, more contemporary psychiatrists such as Laing (1967), Van Dusen (1972), and Ornstein (1972) have developed further this idea that, as the latter puts it, "ordinary" consciousness is a personal construction.

The idea is phrased well by Cambridge philosopher C. D. Broad, who makes the suggestion, following Henri Bergson, that

> . . . the function of the brain and nervous system and sense organs is in the main *eliminative* and not productive. Each person is at each moment capable of remembering all that has ever happened to him and of perceiving everything that is happening everywhere in the universe. The function of

the brain and nervous system is to protect
us from being overwhelmed and confused
by this mass of largely useless and irrelevant
knowledge, by shutting out most of what we
should otherwise perceive or remember at any
moment, and leaving only that very small and
special selection which is likely to be prac-
tically useful. (Quoted in Huxley, 1963, pp.
22-23).

Aldous Huxley comments that

according to such a theory, each one of us is
potentially Mind at Large. But in so far as we
are animals, our business is at all costs to be
funneled through the *reducing valve of the
brain* and nervous system. What comes out at
the other end is a *measly trickle* of the kind
of consciousness which will help us to stay
alive on the surface of this particular planet.
To formulate and express the contents of this
reduced awareness, man has invented and end-
lessly elaborated those symbol-systems and
implicit philosophies which we call languages
. . . That which. . . is called 'this world' is
the *universe of reduced awareness*, expressed,
and as it were, petrified by language. The
various 'other worlds', with which human
beings erratically make contact are so many
elements in the totality of the awareness
belonging to Mind at Large. Most people,
most of the time, know only what comes

through the reducing valve and is consecrated
as genuinely real by the local language. (*Ibid.*
pp. 23-4. My emphasis).

The results of this "reductive" functioning of
perception and thought is to produce a patheti-
cally self-limiting and pathological creature
known as the Average Person. This is forcefully
stated by R. D. Laing, one of the most influential figures in the "anti-psychiatry" movement of the 60's and 70's.

> Our capacity to think, except in the service of
> what we are dangerously deluded in supposing
> is our self-interest and in conformity with
> common sense, is pitifully limited: our ca-
> pacity even to see, hear, touch, taste and smell
> is so shrouded in veils of mystification that an
> intensive discipline of unlearning is necessary
> for anyone before one can begin to experience
> the world afresh, with innocence, truth and
> love.
>
> And immediate experience of, in contrast
> to belief or faith in, a spiritual realm of de-
> mons, spirits, Powers, Dominions, Principali-
> ties, Seraphim, and Cherubim, the Light, is
> even more remote. As domains of experience
> become more alien to us, we need greater
> open-mindedness even to conceive of their
> existence.
>
> Many of us do not know, or even believe,

that every night we enter zones of reality in
which we forget our waking life as regularly
as we forget our dreams when we awake. . .
Many (psychologists). . . believe that fantasy
is the farthest that experience goes under
'normal' circumstances. Beyond that are simple 'pathological' zones of hallucinations, phan-
tasmagoric mirages, delusions.

This state of affairs represents an almost un-
believable devastation of our experience. . .
What we call 'normal' is a product of re-
pression, denial, splitting projection, intro-
jection and other forms of destructive action
on experience. . . It is radically estranged from
the structure of being.

. . . The condition of alienation, of being
asleep, of being unconscious, or being out of
one's mind, is the condition of the normal
man. (Laing, 1967. pp. 26-8. My emphasis).

There are four essential modes of by-passing
the reduction valve systems of our ordinary mental and perceptual functioning: mortality, madness, medicine, and meditation. The first three
will be touched on briefly below. The fourth,
meditation, will be dealt with in a subsequent
chapter.

MORTALITY—Traditional spiritual teaching systems have long maintained the existence of a conscious entity before physical birth and after

bodily death. Some contemporary scientists are beginning to agree. The best known is perhaps Dr. Elisabeth Kubler-Ross, a specialist in the psychiatry of terminal illness. She has assembled a body of testimony from patients who have been enabled to survive the experience of "clinical" death by modern techniques of resuscitation. She states,

> I have investigated similar cases from Australia to California, involving patients from age 2 to 96—I have 193 clear-cut cases from all over the world, both religious and non religious people. One had been 'dead' twelve and one-half hours. All experienced the same thing. . . peace, no pain, no anxiety. . . Not one of them was afraid to die again. The experience seems to be the same no matter what their cultural background.
>
> After the transition, you achieve a higher understanding which includes a review of your own life. You see all the times you should have acted one way and acted another, all the times you regret. It is not God who has to convince you of your wrongs; it is you yourself, and it is hell. . .
>
> I know for a fact there is life after death. . . (Witt, 1975, pp. 66-7).

Psychologist Lawrence LeShan has examined the question of 'human survival of biological death' in the context of field theory in contemporary physics. He concludes,

> Organizing the world in the manner of classical physics leads inexorably to the conclusion that biological death means total annihilation (nonexistence) of the individual. Organizing the world in the manner of field theory leads as inexorably to a conclusion of survival of biological death. (Le Shan, 1974).

MADNESS—It is clear that the concepts of 'sanity' and 'madness' have undergone a rather total reevaluation, if not a devaluation, in current psychiatric thought. Those modes of experience that were arbitrarily designated as outside the realm of 'sanity' by conventional standards, both popular and psychiatric, are increasingly seen as either (a) independent 'realities' in themselves, or as (b) natural avenues toward psychological integration and health. Visions, voices, dreams, fantasies and 'peak experiences' are being taken seriously by many contemporary psychotherapists, not only in other people, but in themselves.

One such practitioner is Wilson VanDusen who sees such experiences as indicators of what he calls the 'natural depth of man'. Contact with this natural depth may be therapeutic or traumatic for the individual depending in part on his or her preparation for it, and also on the way in which the resulting experiences are defined both for the experiencer and by others. As Van Dusen sees it,

> The personal identity and history on the superficial level of consciousness deepen into the innate, natural tendencies. It is as though in the depth is the main part of ourselves and the depth leads the individual *through* the circumstances of his life *along* the lines of his innate tendencies. This is the Way for the individual. The felt freedom of the individual increases along this Way. The possible dramas include all human dramas, and especially all those needed by the individual to perfect him. The simple bounds of self are broken open to include all selves, under all circumstances, through all time. Indeed, the bounds break open beyond humanness to include all life and even the material world. (VanDusen, 1972, pp. 205-6).

The necessity of a knowledgeable guide to such experience is implicit in this view. Laing gives his vision of the way in which the cultivation of inner experience might be facilitated instead of devalued.

> . . . we need a place where people. . . can

find their way *further* into inner space and time, and back again. Instead of the *degradation* ceremonial of psychiatric examination, diagnosis and prognostication, we need, for those who are ready for it (in psychiatric terminology, often those who are about to go into a schizophrenic breakdown), an *initiation* ceremonial, through which the person will be guided with full social encouragement and sanction into inner space and time, by people who have been there and back again. Psychiatrically, this would appear as ex-patients helping future patients to go mad.

What is entailed then is:

    (1) a voyage from outer to inner,

    (2) from life to a kind of death,

    (3) from going forward to going back

    (4) from temporal movement to temporal standstill

    (5) from mundane time to eonic time

    (6) from the ego to the self

    (7) from outside (post-birth) back into the womb of all things (pre birth)

and then subsequently a return voyage from

    (1) inner to outer

    (2) from death to life

    (3) from the movement back to a movement once more forward

> (4) from immortality back to mortality,
> (5) from eternity back to time,
> (6) from self to a new ego,
> (7) from a cosmic fetalization to an existential rebirth.
>
> . . . This process could have a central function in a truly sane society. (Laing, 1967, pp. 128-9).

There is a striking parallel between Laing's dual seven-stage journey inward and the archetypal form of all primitive rites of passage, popular hero myths, ancient and modern, the initiation rituals of all religions and the course of individual growth experienced by masters of all the traditional spiritual growth systems. Joseph Campbell, following James Joyce, has dubbed this archetypal form the 'Monomyth' and has shown that it comprises the three stages of: separation, initiation and return. As Campbell summarizes it:

> A hero ventures forth from the world of common day into a region of supernatural wonder; fabulous forces are there encountered and a decisive victory is won: the hero comes back from this mysterious adventure with the power to bestow boons on his fellow man. (Campbell, 1949, p. 30).

As Campbell outlines it, the archetypal journey of
everyman looks like this:

Separation or Departure

(1) The call to 'Adventure', or the
     signs of the vocation of the 'hero'
(2) Refusal of the Call, or the folly
     of the flight from the god
(3) Supernatural Aid, the unsuspected
     assistance that comes to one who
     has undertaken his proper adven-
     ture. ['when the chela is ready, the
     master appears']
(4) The Crossing of the First Threshold
(5) The Belly of the Whale, or the
     passage into the realm of night.

Initiation: Trials and Victories

(1) The road of Trials, or the danger-
     ous aspect of the gods
(2) The Meeting with the Goddess
     (Magna Mater), or the bliss of
     infancy regained
(3) Woman as the Temptress [or in
     less sexist terms, the Stage of
     Temptations]
(4) Atonement with the Father
(5) Apotheosis [elevation to godly
     rank]

(6) The Ultimate Boon [Enlighten-
      ment

The Return and Integration with Society

(1) Refusal of the Return, or the
      world denied
(2) The Magic Flight. . .
(3) Rescue from Without
(4) The Crossing of the Return Thres-
      old, or the return to the world of
      common day
(5) Master of the Two Worlds
(6) Freedom to Live [and bring the
      ultimate boon to others, the
      Bodhisattva ideal]

(*Ibid*., pp. 36-7).

All saints at some point in their development
spend a period in the "desert"—out of the world.
After realization, however, there is a pattern of
return or social re-entry; of, as Swami Rama
phrases it, "becoming creative in the world" for
the good of others.

Thus does the 20th century psychiatric paradigm move toward convergence with the timeless
order of the initiation process.

MEDICINE—The use of chemical substances,
natural and synthetic, to short-circuit the reduc-
tion-filter of the brain and senses is by no means

unique to the psychedelic sixties. Human attempts to take short cuts to extraordinary experience are no doubt as old as the race itself. Despite the popular hysteria both pro and con caused by the widespread use in recent years of altering drugs, a few serious and responsible scientists have used them for the judicious exploration of some little-understood forms of human consciousness.

One such researcher is Stanislov Grof, a Czechoslovakian psychiatrist now working in the United States. For the past 17 years Dr. Grof has been amassing observations based on over 3000 sessions in which patients were administered LSD and other psychedelic substances under carefully controlled conditions (Grof, 1973). Whatever one's attitude toward the use of psychedelics in a psychiatric context, the fact remains that Grof has been one of the major contributors with Anthony Sutich, Charles Tart, John Lilly, the Greens, and others, to the establishment of Transpersonal Psychology and the experimental 'mapping' of human consciousness.[3]

Based on his collected data, Grof has developed an influential typology of inner experience (Ring, 1974). It is outlined briefly here because of its importance to the evolving psychiatric paradigm and its relevance to our study.

A. Ontogenetic or Perinatal experiences—
    remembered from or related to stages in
    the embryonic development and birth
    process of the individual.

> 1. Cosmic Unity, 'Good Womb',
>   symbiotic oneness with the envi-
>   ronment, "Eternity now/Infinity
>   here"
>
> 2. Cosmic Engulfment, "Bad Womb"
>   Onset of delivery
>
> 3. "No Exit" or hell, contractions of
>   the uterus have begun, cervix re-
>   mains closed
>
> 4. Death-Rebirth struggles
>
> 5. Embryonal and Fetal Experiences
>   Types two through four bring the ex-
>   periencer forcefully in contact with
>   human finitude and the vulnerability
>   of biological existence.

According to Grof (1973, p. 25), "the individual comes to realize through these experiences that no matter what he does in his life, he
cannot escape the inevitable: he will have to
leave this world bereft of everything that he has
accumulated, achieved and has been emotion-
ally attached to. The similarity between birth
and death—the startling realization that the
beginning of life is the same as its end—is the
major philosophical issue that accompanies the

perinatal experiences. The other important consequence of the shocking emotional and physical encounter with the phenomenon of death is the opening up of spiritual and religious dimensions that appear to be an intrinsic part of the human personality; and programming. . . Even the most hard-core materialists . . . become suddenly interested in spiritual search after they confronted these levels in themselves.''

B. Trans-individual experiences
   1. Ancestral—family, ethnic, racial, and trans-racial 'memories'
   2. Past incarnations
   3. Archetypal, trans-cultural symbolic elements

C. Phylogenetic experiences (not necessarily in ascending order)
   1. Inorganic matter consciousness
   2. Organ, tissue and cellular consciousness
   3. Plant
   4. Animal
   5. Planetary
   6. Oneness with life and creation

D. Extraterrestrial

> Experiences of apparent contact with
> super-human and sub-human spiritual
> entities.
> E. The Void
> > "It is beyond time and space, beyond
> > change, and beyond polarities such as
> > good and evil, light and darkness, sta-
> > bility and motion, agony and ecstasy."
> > (Grof, 1972, p. 75).

Glimpses of this category of experiences are
very rare and fleeting in psycholytic research. As
Alpert/Ram Dass (1974) has reported from his
own experience, there are no chemical shortcuts
to lasting higher consciousness.

On the basis of his research, Grof concludes,

> *The model of personality and image of man*
> *emerging is much closer to Hindu philosophy*
> *than to the Freudian concepts* that are at
> present widely accepted by western science
> and philosophy. . . The general picture of
> human personality as depicted by the Hindus
> shows the human mind as a multi-layered dy-
> namic structure with elements of the individu-
> al and collective unconsciousness, as well as
> karmic and ancient evolutionary (phylogenetic)
> memories buried in its depths. From this point
> of view, even the "depth pyschological" ap-
> proach of classical and neoclassical Freudian

analysis barely scratches the surface. . .
Ultimately, *the final frontiers of the human
mind appear to coincide with those of the
universe.* (Paradoxically, the most recent discoveries in the area of mind research seem to
coincide with concepts developed several
thousand years ago. . . Strangely enough, the
new concepts of consciousness and the human
mind are also quite compatible with evolu-
tionary theory. . . and with some recent
developments of modern physics, such as Einstein's unified field theory. . . and quantum
mechanics. . . (Grof, 1973, pp. 38-9. My
emphasis).

All of which is another way of phrasing the
recurring human insights into the nature of mind,
self and reality that Aldous Huxley has called
"Perennial Philosophy". He describes it like this:

Philosophia perennia—the phrase coined by
Leibnitz; but the thing—the metaphysic that
recognizes a divine Reality substantial to the
world of things and lives and minds; the
psychology that finds in the soul something
similar to, or even identical with, divine Reality; the ethic that places man's final end in the
knowledge of the immanent and transcendent
Ground of all being—the thing is immemorial
and universal. Rudiments of the Perennial
Philosophy may be found among the tradi-
tionary lore of primitive peoples in every

region of the world, and in its fully developed form it has a place in every one of the higher religions. A version of this Highest Common Factor in all preceding and subsequent theologies was first committed to writing more than twenty-five centuries ago (in Sanskrit; the Vedas), and since that time the inexhaustible theme has been treated again and again, from the standpoint of every religious tradition and in all the principle languages of Asia and Europe. (Huxley, 1945, p. vii).

As we have seen, we may now add to this catalogue of languages those of contemporary science.

Mystical Science and Scientific Mysticism: Convergence and Divergence

Convergence

The world view that emerges from the shifting paradigm of 20th century science looks something like this:

There is no objective perceptual reality. Since science is based on data supplied by technological extensions of the human sensory apparatus, and since the human senses are a system of reducing valves sealing us off from the pleroma of possible experiences, human knowledge based on perception is limited and uncertain.

There is no objective social self. The 'emperical' ego is a function of mis-identification with a bundle of shifting social roles and experiential modes. As one might say, *ego ergo ignorance.*

Consciousness is the only constant and creates everything else. Each "individual" is a node or localization of consciousness through which mind-at-large seeks to be conscious simultaneously of its creations and of itself. The "realized" person free of ego, is the mask through which the universal sounds (per-sona); the "Master of Two Worlds"; Janus, the two-faced, looking outward and inward at the same time. As Lama Govinda puts it, it is not that the drop enters the ocean, but that the ocean enters the drop. (Govinda, 1975).

In humans, consciousness may be 'mapped' as shown in the diagram following. It is important to remember, however, that as Korzybski warns, "The map is not the territory." It is for purposes of the present discussion only.

SUPERCONSCIOUS
(stages in the experience of "monistic" mysticism) the One, the Void, Consciousness Without Object

waking
sleeping
dreaming
fantasizing

access to:

"NORMAL" CONSCIOUSNESS

Pre-conscious or subconscious (Freudian) psychodynamic or unconscious (Jungian) ontogenetic experience

Realm of:
extra-normal parapsychological, phylogenetic, and "Pluralistic" mystical experiences of unity with phenomenal forms.

As the Greens following Aurobindo, have pointed out (1971b), the expansion of consciousness can be thought of as occurring not only vertically—upward and downward—but horizontally or tangentially as well. This would help explain the apparent occurrence of two seemingly opposed modes of mystical experience—unity with the forms of becoming and unity with formless being—that has confused some scholars of comparative mysticism (Otto, 1957; Zaehner, 1961). It also helps explain the bankruptcy of Western psychologies whose direction in terms of this map is "down and out", in comparison with Eastern psychologies whose direction is "out and up".

In any event, our ultimate concern is with the superconscious section of the map—and not merely with demonstrating its existence, but with experiencing it directly. Here is where the recent "mystical" science of the West and the scientific "mysticism" of the East part company.

Divergence

The Danish existentialist Soren Kierkegaard once made fun of the German philosopher Hegel for constructing a glorious palace of metaphysical thought and continuing to live his life next door in the pathetic hovel of everyday consciousness. The contemporary scientist can be said to be in much the same position with regard to ultimate reality. He has satisfied himself of its presence and probable nature, but how is he to experience it? His technological sense extensions and rational modes of inquiry do not bring him any closer to direct participatory consciousness of reality than is the 'normal' man or woman in the street. Thus, like Moses, the scientist can lead others (intellectually, at least) toward the 'promised land', but cannot enter it himself—unless, that is, he makes the step from secular science to the science of the sacred and becomes the subject of his own experiment.

The two modes are not opposed, merely different. One contemporary physicist sees them ". . . as two complementary manifestations of the human mind; of its rational and intuitive faculties . . . both of them are necessary for a fuller understanding of the world. . . " (Capra, 1975).

But for the experiential knowing of the self-beyond-the-world only one mode will suffice—the science of the cultivation of consciousness: meditation.

NOTES

[1]One of the main reasons for the reluctance of eastern masters to perform such feats for western scientists has surely been the traditional yogic injunction against the display of the powers, or *siddhis,* which are developed as side effects of their methods of spiritual culture. Public exhibition of the *siddhis* except for unselfish purposes is seen as a dangerous hinderance to further growth on the part of the practitioner. In taking part in the Green's experiments Swami Rama was acting on the instructions of his own spiritual teacher to facilitate a rapprochement between the eastern and western approaches to psychology. Such events may well be considered child's play by yogis except in a laboratory setting; "Unless you see signs and wonders, you will not believe."

[2]All quotations in this group are from the collection of LeShan, 1974 except for "B" and "H" which are from Toben, 1975 and "L", which is from Capra, 1975. The sources of the quotations are, respectively. A—Vivekananda; B—John Wheeler, physicist; C—Eddington, physicist; D—the Suringama Sutra; E—Evelyn Underhill, mystic; F—Schrodinger, physicist; G—Plotinus, mystic; H—Wheeler, physicist; I—Shvetashvatara Upanishad; J—Aurobindo, mystic; K—Max Planck, physicist; L—Lama Anagarika Govinda.

[3]Transpersonal or 'Fourth Force' psychology,—after psychoanalytic, behavioristic and humanistic or 'Third Force' psychologies—is concerned with studying and

facilitating experience beyond ego, space and time. "Transpersonal" Therapy is concerned with the psychological processes related to the realization (i.e. making real) of such states as 'illumination', 'Mystical union', 'transcendence', 'cosmic unity', etc., as well as concerned with the psychological conditions or psychodynamic processes that are directly or indirectly a barrier to such transpersonal realizations." (Sutich, 1973, p.3)

BIBLIOGRAPHY

Brown, Barbara B. & Joy W. Klug, *The Alpha Syllabus: A Handbook of Human EEG Activity*, Charles C. Thomas, Springfield, Ill., 1974, A.

Brown, Barbara B. *New Mind, New Body; Bio-Feedback: New Direction for the Mind*, Harper & Row, 1974, B.

Campbell, Joseph, *The Hero with a Thousand Faces*, Meridan Books, World Pub. Co., New York, 1949.

Capra, Fritjof, "The Cosmic Web of Physicists and Mystics", *East West Journal*, Vol. 5, No. 11, Nov. 15, 1975, pp. 32-5.

Chesterton, John, *et al*, Collectively known as the Catalogue, *An Index of Possibilities: Energy & Power*, Pantheon Books/Random House, New York, 1974.

Dass, Ram, Ram Dass lecture at the Maryland Psychiatric Research Center, R. I.

Dass, Ram, *The only Dance There Is*, Anchor, 1974.

Fuller, R. Buckminister, *Synergetics: Exploration in the Geometry of Thinking*, 1975.

Goyandka, Jayadayal, Jr, *The Bhagavadgita or The Song Divine*, Gita Press, 1973.

Green, Elmer E., Alyce Green, E. Dale Walters, "Biofeedback for

Mind-Body Self-Regulation: Healing and Creativity", Research Dept., The Menninger Foundation. Oct. 30, 1971 a.

Green, Elmer E. & Alyce M. Green, "On the Meaning of Transpersonal: Some Metaphysical Perspectives", *Journal of Transpersonal Psychology*, 1971, b, 27-41.

Green, Elmer E., Alyce Green, "The Ins & Outs of Mind-Body Energy, *The world Book Science Annual*, 1974.

Grof, Stanislav, "Varieties of Transpersonal Experiences—Observations from LSD Research", *Journal of Transpersonal Psychology*, Stanford, Ca. 1973, Vol. 5, no. 1.

Grof, Stanislav, "Theoretical & Emporical Basis of Transpersonal Psychology & Psychotherapy: Observations from LSD Research", *Journal of Transpersonal Psychology*, Stanford, Ca., 1973, Vol. 5, no. 1.

Grun, Bernard, *The Time Tables of History*, Simon & Schuster, New York, 1975.

Harman, Willis, "The New Copernican Revolution", *Future Conditional*, 1969.

Hawken, Paul, *The Magic of Findhorn*, Harper & Row, New York, 1975.

Huxley, Aldous, *The Perennial Philosophy*, Harper, 1945.

Huxley, Aldous, *Door of Perception/Heaven and Hell*, Harper/New American Library, 1958.

James, William, *The Varieties of Religious Experience*, Mentor/New American Library, 1958.

Koestler, Arthur, *The Roots of Coincidence*, Random House, New York, 1972.

Kuhn, Thomas S., *The Structure of Scientific Revolutions*, University of Chicago Press, Chicago, Ill. 1970.

Laing, R. D., *The Politics of Experience*, Ballantine Books, New

York, 1967.

LeShan, Lawrence, *The Medium, The Mystic, & The Physicist: Toward a Theory of the Paranormal*, Viking, New York, 1974.

Lilly, John C., *The Center of the Cyclone*, The Julian Press, New York, 1972.

Mishlove, Jeffrey, *The Roots of Consciousness*, Random House, Bookworks, 1975.

Monroe, Robert A., *Journeys Out of the Body*, Doubleday/Anchor, New York, 1973.

Moss, Thelma, *The Probability of the Impossible*, J. P. Tarcher, Inc., Los Angeles, 1974.

Ornstein, Robert E., *The Psychology of Consciousness*, W. H. Freemen & Company, San Francisco, 1972.

Otto, Rudolph, *Mysticism East & West: A comparative Analysis of the Nature of Mysticism*, Meridan Books, New York, 1957.

Rama, Swami, *Book of Wisdom (Ishopanishad)*, Himalayan International Institute, Chicago, 1972.

Rama, Swami, *Lectures on Yoga*, Himalayan International Institute, Glenview, Illinois, 1973.

Rieker, Hans-Ulrich, *The Secret of Meditation*, The Philosophical Library, New York, 1957.

Ring, Kennith, "A Transpersonal View of Consciousness: A Mapping of Farther Reaches of Inner Space", *Journal of Transpersonal Psychology*, Stanford, Ca., 1974.

Smith, Sister Mary Justice, *The Ultimate Mystery*, Hartley Productions, Cos Cob, Conn., 1974.

Sutich, Anthony J., "Transpersonal Therapy", *Journal of Transpersonal Psychology*, Vol. 5, no. 1, 1973.

Tart, Charles T., *Altered States of Consciousness*, Doubleday Anchor Books, 1972.

Toben, Bob, with Jack Sarfatti & Fred Wolf, *Space Time and Beyond*: Toward an Explanation of the Unexplainable, Dutton, New York, 1975.

Tompkins, Peter & Christopher Bird, *The Secret Life of Plants*, Harper & Row, New York, 1973.

Vandusen, Wilson, *The Natural Depth in Man*, Perennial Library, Harper & Row, New York, 1972.

Watts, Allan, *Psychotherapy East & West*, Mentor, Random House, 1961.

Weide, Thomas, N. "Council Grove IV: Toward a Science of Ultimates", *Journal of Transpersonal Psychology*, Stanford, Calif. 1972, Vol. 4, No. 1.

Witt, Linda, "Interview with Dr. Elizabeth Kubler-Ross", *People* Magazine, November 24, 1975, pp. 66-69.

Yogananda, Paramahansa, *Autobiography of a Yogi*, Jaico Publishing House, Doubleday, 1972.

Zaeher, R. C., *Mysticism, Sacred & Profane*, Galaxy Books, Oxford University Press, 1961.

Achievement in Meditation

L. K. MISRA, Ph.D.

Dr. L. K. Misra, Director of the Himalayan Institute in Kanpur, India, is an expert in systems of Indian philosophy. He has written many books in the fields of philosophy and psychology. Dr. Misra was director of several national conferences on Vedanta and Yoga in India and has travelled widely throughout India with many great Saints and Sages.

Dr. Misra was especially trained and initiated by Sri Swami Rama in the tradition of the long line of sages which is one of the most ancient yogic traditions of the Himalayas.

Currently residing in the United States, he is conducting lecture series at the Institute and affiliated Centers. His subjects include yoga psychology, meditation, yoga sutras and, most notably, Sadhana, in which he explains and emphasizes the application of various sadhana practices in daily life.

In the classical book on the philosophy and psychology of Yoga, Patanjali describes three different states of consciousness, which are experienced by ordinary human beings. But there is one more higher state of consciousness: *Turiya*, which is only experienced by doing deep meditation. The *Turiya* state of consciousness is beyond these three states and is the source of transpersonal experiences. Modern psychology has tried to explain this transpersonal phenomenon of consciousness but has failed in giving an accurate picture of this state.

In the third chapter of *Yoga Sutras*, the *Vibhuti Pada*, Patanjali gives a vivid description of the different achievements of one who is adept in achieving the state of *Samadhi*. *Dharana, Dhyana and Samadhi* are called "internal" ways of spiritual practice. For a person who has gone deeper into *Samadhi*, the hidden treasure of inner life is manifested. The personality of that person is transformed, and he becomes enlightened from within and without. In the words of Claudio Naranjo, "If its medium is movement, it will turn into dance; if it is stillness, into living sculpture; if thinking, into the higher reaches of intuition; if sensing, into a merging with the miracle of being; if feeling, into love; if singing, into sacred utterance; if speaking, into prayer or poetry; if doing the things of ordinary life, into a ritual in the name of God, or a celebration of existence." When a person attains this higher state of consciousness, his total personality is transformed, and he develops a complete harmony and equilibrium.

In the *Vibhuti Pada* of *Yoga Sutras*, Patanjali mentions different disciplines, *"sanyama".* When a yogi has attained *Samprajnata Samadhi* he establishes himself in the Higher Consciousness and the pure awareness of reality is established. He gradually develops one-pointedness and remains tranquil despite all the distractions of life.

Patanjali mentions three kinds of transformations: *nirodha, samadhi,* and *ekagrata.* When a yogi disciplines his mind with respect to all these transformations, he receives knowledge of the

past and future.   It is difficult to verify the
Siddhis mentioned by Patanjali from the modern
scientific point of view.   For an ordinary man,
these *Siddhis* are regarded as miraculous or supernatural powers, but yogis do not take the slightest
pleasure or pride in the exercise of occult powers
which they possess.   Yogis attach no importance
to these miraculous powers or *siddhis*; rather,
they have discarded them for the sake of spiritual
attainment.

Patanjali himself has not given any detailed
description of these *Siddhis*, but he has described
in the *Vibhuti Pada* a few of the important ones.
By performing *Sanyama* on sound, a yogi compre-
hends the meanings of sounds uttered by any
living being.   A yogi attains knowledge of previous birth if he focuses his mind on the impres-
sions of life.   If he concentrates on the image
occupying the mind, he attains knowledge of the
minds of others.   By performing *Sanyama* on
Rupa (form) the contact between the eye and
light is broken, and the body becomes invisible.
The same power can be attained with respect to
sound, etc.   When a yogi performs *Sanyama* on
two kinds of *karma,* active and dormant, he
attains knowledge of the time of death.   By
directing the light of the superphysical faculty,
he attains knowledge of small, hidden, and dis-

tant objects. By performing *Sanyama* on the moon, knowledge concerning the arrangement of the stars is attained. By performing *Sanyama* on the navel center, he attains knowledge of the organization of the body and all the physiological functions. By performing *Sanyama* on the gullet, cessation of hunger and thirst is achieved. By performing *Sanyama* on the *Kurmanadi*, he attains steadiness. By performing *Sanyama* on the *Ajna Chakra*, he attains visions of perfected beings. By performing *Sanyama* on the heart, awareness of the nature of the mind is attained. When a yogi performs *Sanyama* on the Self, he attains knowledge of the *Purusha*, and then intuitional hearing, touch, sight, taste and smell are achieved.

The above description gives only a glimpse of the supernatural powers, or *Siddhis*, but Patanjali himself has abandoned them for the sake of spiritual attainment. He says these are obstacles on the path of highest wisdom.

In the last part of the *Vibhuti Pada*, Patanjali further explains other kinds of *Siddhis*. By attaining mastery over *Udana*, levitation and non-contact with water, mire, ponds, etc. are attained. By mastery over *Samana*, blazing of gastric fire is attained. By performing *Sanyama* on the relation between *Akasha* and the ear, superphysical hearing is attained. By performing *Sanyama* on the gross, constant, subtle, all-pervading and functional states of *Panchabhuta*, five elements, a yogi attains complete control of them. After perfecting *Sanyama* on these elements, a yogi attains eight kinds of *Siddhis: Anima, Mahima, Laghima, Garima, Prapti, Prakamya, Ishatwa* and *Vasittva.* With all these *Siddhis*, he receives perfection of the physical body, he attains beauty, fine complexion, strength and adamantine hardness which constitute perfection of the body. He also attains mastery over the sense organs by performing *Sanyama* on their power of cognition, real nature, egoism, all-pervasiveness, and functions.

According to Patanjali, the ultimate goal of life is to attain *Kaivalya*, or Liberation. For attainment of this highest goal of life, a yogi should avoid pleasure or temptation on being invited by the superphysical entities in charge of various planes, because there is still the possibility of the revival of evil.

The highest knowledge, born of the awareness of Reality, is transcendant. It includes the cognition of all objects simultaneously, pertains to all objects and processes whatsoever in the past, present, and future, and transcends the world process. *Kaivalya*, or Liberation, is attained when there is equilibrium of purity between the *Puru-sha* and *Sattva*. *(Yoga Sutras III, 56).*

It is evident from the above description that, according to the classical text on the subject, the first and most important need of a yogi is to attain *Kaivalya*. All other attainments are secondary, and they should not be displayed for the sake of any personal attainment. For ordinary human understanding, these yogic phenomena cannot be explained in scientific terms and it is difficult to verify them objectively. The mind of modern man is not satisfied with all these supernatural powers unless they are verified by scientists. Scientific investigation needs an analytical approach towards the problems of human life, but this has its limitations. Science cannot cross these limits, and it is therefore impossible for it to investigate any of the phenomena of the transpersonal state of human consciousness. All the facts about these supernatural powers can be understood only when a person himself becomes adept in these supernatural powers, through the practice of deep meditation for several years.

For a long time, this art and science of Yoga and Meditation was hidden, and only a few sincere persons seeking the real knowledge of Yoga and Meditation could achieve something from the tradition of the great masters. Modern man has now become conscious of this art and science of Yoga and Meditation. In this age of trial and turmoil and materialistic approaches to life, man wants to understand the real implication of this knowledge. With the help of a few masters in Yoga and Meditation, modern scientists and doctors are beginning to investigate the efficacy of this knowledge. They are finding that this knowledge of Yoga and Meditation develops better understanding within each of us for the problems of life. When a person regularly meditates, his mind becomes balanced, and he enjoys equilibrium and peace. He receives strength to remain apart from all the emotional problems of life. He is established in the truth of the Self, and he understands perfectly the goal of his life. After practicing meditation for a considerable time, a person achieves coordination and harmony between the inner and outer self; it becomes possible for him to unfold knowledge previously hidden in the unconscious mind. He establishes himself in knowledge of the real Self through the practice of meditation.

The practice of meditation gives the power of understanding, so that one can face all the problems of life with equilibrium and harmony. Meditation is an effortless process, and it can be attained here and now. If there is anything in the

mind of the meditator which relates to the past
or the future, he loses the glory of meditation. A
person approached the Buddha with offerings of
flowers in both hands. The Buddha said, "Drop
it." The person dropped the flowers in his left
hand. The Buddha said again, "Drop it." Then
he dropped the flowers in his right hand. And the
Buddha said again, "Drop that which you have
neither in the right nor in the left, but in the middle." The man was instantly enlightened. This
teaching of Lord Buddha explains that the meditator has to catch hold of that state of the mind
which is neither related to the past nor the future. Alan Watts beautifully explains this idea in
his book, *The Way of Zen*: "In watching, just
watch; in sitting, just sit. Above all, don't wob-
ble." Our attachment with the past or the future
does not allow us to be present with the present.
Most of the time, we are present in the past or
the future, and that is why it becomes difficult
for us to meditate and to grasp reality.

Modern psychologists and doctors have tried
to understand the intricacies of *Sanskara* and
Karma. But, instead of using those classical
names of Sanskrit literature, they have put these
terms under new categories, like defense-mechan-
ism, self-system, cognition, motivation, and conditioning. Modern thinkers like Wilhelm Reich,

Fritz Perls, Alexander Lowan and Alpesso see the mind and body in terms of psycho-physiological principles; that every change in the physiological state is accompanied by an appropriate change in the mental-emotional state, and vice-versa. But when the person has reached a total awakening of Reality, Western psychology no longer is adequate to understand him. For psychological theory is based on, and generated by, beings who are, in a sense, asleep, not awake. This state of consciousness where a person is fully aware of external states is called by yogis, sleepless sleep, and these modern scientists cannot comprehend this idea. Lord Buddha has said in the *Dhammapada,* "He whose mind is not fettered by lust and not affected by hate, who has gone beyond both good and evil, for him, the awake, there is no fear." This fearless state is the highest state of the meditator. In this state of consciousness, the meditator becomes free from all his *sanskaras,* and he becomes enlightened.

The ultimate goal of meditation is peace of mind and soul; the understanding and realization of Reality; enlightenment of the highest Truth. But meditation cannot be accepted as the Truth of one aspect of life; it is the totality of all aspects of life, and it can be practiced in silence and in action. When a person practices meditation in silence, he attains peace, understanding, tranquility of mind, a balanced state of consciousness; and when he practices meditation in action, he becomes creative, and his every action of life becomes an action of the Divine. Modern man is not able to grasp all these idealistic thoughts about meditation, and he wants to know the exact result of meditation in his daily life. So modern scientists started experimenting on different aspects of Yoga and Meditation, and in the past few decades they have come to this conclusion: that the achievements of deep meditation are very useful for growth of human consciousness. At the Menninger Research Foundation in Topeka, Kansas, Dr. Elmer Green has conducted studies with Swami Rama of the Himalayas. In his report, Dr. Green clearly concluded that Swami Rama demonstrated the stopping of his heart for seventeen seconds. In another experiment, Swami Rama, while in the state of sleep and producing Delta waves, was able to perceive conversations going on in the room, which he later recalled verbatim. With the modern tools involved in measuring the internal states of meditation, such as Electrocardiographs for measuring heart rate; Spirometers for measuring respiratory rates and ventilation; Electromyographs for recording muscle tone and muscle activity; and

Electroencephalographs for recording brain wave patterns, these scientists are trying to measure the achievements of meditation. But these scientific tools can measure only functions of the body and to a certain extent, the brain. But they are not able to record the subtle vibrations of the mind where the person gets the tremendous power through concentration of the mind on certain objects or *mantra*. Science has yet to invent tools to measure this tremendous power of the mind which is not easily recordable nor understandable through their present equipment. No doubt, these scientists have proven that meditation has wonderful effects in the body and mind of the human being, and, if it is properly practiced, it can really transform their life, but Science has yet to verify the results of meditation as described by Patanjali in the *Vibhuti Pada* of his *Yoga Sutras*. The description given by Patanjali seems idealistic and unapproachable but when we see the results of modern experiments conducted on a few great yogis, we can have no doubt about the achievements of these great masters.

This art and science of Meditation has proved its worth, and for a man of understanding there is no doubt that the practice of Meditation transforms the total personality, and the person has a better perspective of life in all its aspects, including emotional factors and ideological conflicts. Meditation is a boat for crossing the River of Life.

References

Chaudhuri, Haridas, *Philosophy of Meditation*, New York: Philosophical Library, 1965.

Naranjo, Claudio, *On the Psychology of Meditation*, New York: An Essalen Book, 1972.

Swami Rama, R. Ballentine, and Swami Ajaya, *Yoga and Psychotherapy*, Glenview: The Himalayan Institute, 1976.

Taimni, I. K., *The Science of Yoga*, Wheaton: Theosophical Publishing House, 1961.

White, John, ed., *What is Meditation?*, New York: Anchor Books, 1974.

BOOKS PUBLISHED BY THE HIMALAYAN INSTITUTE

Yoga and Psychotherapy	Swami Rama, R. Ballentine, M.D. Swami Ajaya
Emotion to Enlightenment	Swami Rama, Swami Ajaya
Freedom from the Bondage of Karma	Swami Rama
Book of Wisdom—Ishopanishad	Swami Rama
Lectures on Yoga	Swami Rama
Life Here and Hereafter	Swami Rama
Marriage, Parenthood & Enlightenment	Swami Rama
Meditation in Christianity	Swami Rama et al.
Superconscious Meditation	Usharbudh Arya, Ph.D.
Philosophy of Hatha Yoga	Usharbudh Arya, Ph.D.
Yoga Psychology	Swami Ajaya
Living with the Himalayan Masters	Swami Ajaya (ed)
Psychology East and West	Swami Ajaya (ed)
Foundations of Eastern & Western Psychology	Swami Ajaya (ed)
Meditational Therapy	Swami Ajaya (ed)
Art & Science of Meditation	L. K. Misra, Ph.D. (ed)
Swami Rama of the Himalayas	L. K. Misra, Ph.D. (ed)
Theory & Practice of Meditation	R. Ballentine, M.D. (ed)
Science of Breath	R. Ballentine, M.D. (ed)
Joints and Glands Exercises	R. Ballentine, M.D. (ed)
Science Studies Yoga	James Funderburk, Ph.D.
Hatha Yoga Manual I	Samskrti and Veda
Chants for Eternity	Institute Residents
The Swami and Sam (for children)	Brandt Dayton
Himalayan Mountain Cookery	Mrs. R. Ballentine, Sr.
The Yoga Way Cookbook	Friends of the Institute